Beyond compare.
With 963 appearances,
168 goals and 25 major
honours for Manchester
United, Ryan Giggs
enjoyed a playing
career without equal.

# Ryan Giggs

## The Man for All Seasons

Steve Bartram &
Adam Marshall

SIMON &
SCHUSTER

London · New York · Sydney · Toronto · New Delhi

A CBS COMPANY

First published in Great Britain by
Simon & Schuster UK Ltd, 2014
A CBS Company

1 3 5 7 9 10 8 6 4 2

Simon & Schuster UK Ltd
1st Floor
222 Gray's Inn Road
London
WC1X 8HB

www.simonandschuster.co.uk

Simon & Schuster Australia
Sydney

Simon & Schuster India
New Delhi

A CIP catalogue record for this book is available from
the British Library

ISBN: 978-1-47113-990-1

Edited by Julian Flanders
Pages designed by Craig Stevens
Printed and bound in Italy by L.E.G.O. SpA

# Contents

Foreword by Sir Bobby Charlton          7

1   The Boy Who Could Fly               9

2   Breakthrough Act                    31

3   A Roller Coaster Ride               57

4   Toast of the Continent              83

5   Reinventing the Zeal                105

6   Guiding Light                       127

7   Record Breaker                      151

8   The Never-Ending Glory              173

9   Last Man Standing                   203

10  A Twist in the Tale                 229

11  Epilogue by Louis van Gaal          254

Acknowledgements and Picture Credits    256

# Foreword
## by Sir Bobby Charlton

In all honesty, I would have been a little upset if I had not been asked to write the foreword to this book.

I never really thought about my appearances record for Manchester United when I had it, but I certainly did not object to Ryan overtaking it. He deserved it and if I could have chosen for somebody to break it, then it would have been him.

I still remember the first time I clapped eyes on him. I used to go down to The Cliff and Littleton Road, on the other side of the river, where the youngsters trained. You could say I was simply being nosy, but I've always had a keen interest in any players coming through, having enjoyed that same experience many years previously.

The artist Harold Riley lived in Salford and I'd invited him down to have a look around. I knew the manager would not mind, but I arrived early and, instead of waiting for Harold, received a message from Alex Ferguson asking if I would like to watch the new batch of kids we had coming in.

As I made what was a fair walk from the car park, there must have been about ten pitches in front of me and, as I headed towards where Alex was watching, I saw this lad get the ball and, within seconds, he went through and had a shot that just cleared the bar. I thought: 'Cor, who is this little lad?' I found Alex and quickly asked: 'Who was that?' He replied: 'That's Ryan Wilson. We've just signed him this morning, you'll be very pleased to know.'

I knew instantly he was simply one of those unique players. I saw him pick the ball up again and weave around the defenders to find a little bit of space. He cracked in another shot that the goalkeeper

On the evening he relinquished his long-standing club appearances record in Moscow, Sir Bobby Charlton presents Ryan with a watch to commemorate the occasion.

did really well to save. I realised that although he was not a big star yet, he was definitely destined to become one.

At the time, Alex had not been here long since moving down from Scotland. You always worry where the good players are going to come from, but he didn't even have to think about this one – suddenly he'd unearthed a real gem, and left-sided footballers can be hard to find.

Ryan was just sensational and could see everything out on the pitch. He was always aware of what was going on around him and was never afraid to take defenders on. I feel that is something we can be guilty of today, not having a go early enough and passing the ball instead of taking it forward. He always attacked the opposition.

I must confess I never worried when he had the ball. If he was playing, he could save us, even if we were under the cosh, because he could change everything in the blink of an eye. If we needed a goal, he was always capable of coming up trumps – none more so than his solo effort in the 1999 FA Cup semi-final replay with Arsenal – that was just amazing and probably the greatest highlight of his remarkable career.

Manchester United have depended on Ryan to a certain extent for a number of years and have obviously been desperate to keep him in some capacity. He knows the whole club inside out. He's happy, the fans are happy and the club is happy that he remained here after his retirement to become Louis van Gaal's assistant manager.

Ryan possesses such a great attitude to the game and to his fellow players. He's a strong character in general, but always gives you a smile and never seems worried by anything. That is the gift of being a fantastic footballer – playing is the easy part.

Everyone is now looking forward to the future with him in this new role. It will be tough, but he has the ability to adapt and the determination to succeed because he is clearly so immersed in the game.

I have to say Ryan Giggs is an absolute credit to Manchester United. My only fear is we might never find his like again.

# 1

# The Boy Who Could Fly

Watching a 13-year-old Ryan Wilson glide across a football pitch moved Alex Ferguson to evoke comparisons with a cocker spaniel chasing a piece of silver paper in the wind. Had a storyteller prophesied how his career would pan out, it would surely have been dismissed as being pure quixotic fantasy. For all the youngster's extraordinary potential, the level of its fulfilment went beyond the believable. That young pup, later known to the world as Ryan Giggs, would soon be pursuing silverware with an unquenchable thirst that made him the most decorated footballer in British history.

When Giggs finally hung up his boots at the age of forty, he did so with 25 major honours to his name. He could also boast the recent and unexpected honour of managing Manchester United on an interim basis for the final four games of the 2013-14 season. By introducing himself as a substitute against Hull City, on 6 May

# Ryan Giggs
## The Man for All Seasons

2014, the veteran clocked up his 963rd appearance for his one and only professional club. Almost six years had passed since Giggs had overtaken global icon Sir Bobby Charlton as United's all-time leading appearance maker, in the typically romantic setting of a Champions League final victory.

Despite the cautionary warnings of some teachers, who warned against chasing dreams, those with a keen eye could envisage a glorious future for a tall, coltish athlete who had inherited extraordinary speed and balance from his father. Danny Wilson, a Welsh rugby league international, brought his son closer to Old Trafford by leaving Cardiff RFC to sign with Swinton RLFC. The rugby star, whose own father was from Sierra Leone, may have been responsible for the physical prowess of his son, but the player's mother, Lynne, would have the enduring influence over his career, raising the youngster after Danny left home shortly before Ryan's fourteenth birthday.

Giggs officially joined United shortly after his father's departure, but his affiliation with the club was already underway. Timing, as ever, was key to a success story that joined together Giggs, United and the finest manager in the history of British football. At the time of the schoolboy's first trial with United, Ferguson had barely got his feet under the manager's desk after replacing Ron Atkinson a month earlier, in November 1986. 'As soon as I saw him on the pitch over that Christmas period, I knew he was a special footballer,' the Scot stated. 'We set out to make him a Manchester United player.'

Ferguson had rapidly realised the club were losing local talent to neighbours Manchester City and was alarmed to find Wilson was not initially on the radar of the cluster of scouts he had inherited. The Blues had emerged victorious in the FA Youth Cup final between the two clubs in the previous April and five of that City team were to feature in one of the United boss's lowest points in management three years later, inflicting a bruising and humiliating 5-1 thrashing at Maine Road. The tide needed turning.

Ryan's 27-year (and counting) association with United spanned his evolution from teenage talent to assistant manager, and was adorned with more major honours than any other footballer.

'It was perhaps indicative of the state of our scouting system that Ryan didn't join us through normal club channels,' Ferguson later lamented. 'I would have known nothing about Ryan until it was too late, if it hadn't been for one of our stewards, Harold Wood. He came to me soon after I joined the club to ask if I knew of Ryan Wilson, who was then playing for Salford Schools. The answer was no, we didn't know about him. I asked Brian Kidd, who was doing community work in football at that time, and he knew he was training with Manchester City. So I told Joe Brown to get the lad down.'

Brown was the club's youth development officer and was soon in no doubt about the potential of a player blessed with natural speed, skill and stamina. 'In many ways, he's a bit like Tom Finney,' Brown said of the enterprising wide man, 'a natural left-winger that goes for defenders and weaves past them. He's a super lad. I can't find a fault with him as a person or a prospective professional. If he's spared injury and progresses as smoothly as he has done so far, he should become as big a name as Mark Hughes. He is going to be a player that people will want to pay to go to watch.'

Youth team coach Eric Harrison was also assigned with the task of discovering if the hype was justified and, on his first sighting of the winger, felt comfortable making a bold prediction to a new boss who was openly disappointed with the current scouting system. 'I remember seeing him for Salford Boys against Warrington Boys when the manager asked me to take a look at him,' said the Yorkshireman. 'Normally, I take a long time but, after seeing him for ten minutes – I'm not lying – he took my breath away. So I said to Alex: "You don't know me well yet, but I'll stand or fall by this. He will be a Manchester United first-teamer for many years."'

Others within the game had been alerted to the precocious prodigy, including Dave Bushell, later United's Head of Education and Welfare. City had stolen a march on their rivals through their own scout Dennis Schofield, who also happened to be coach of Deans FC,

Professional rugby league player Danny Wilson, Ryan's father, passed on his phenomenal pace and balance.

Giggs joins fellow Greater Manchester schoolboys John Foster and David Hall for a photo-call following the trio's call-up to England Under-15s duty in March 1989.

the local team where Wilson was cutting his teeth as a footballer. However, word was now beginning to get out.

'I saw him when he was twelve or thirteen,' recollected Bushell, who would soon have a direct influence on the local lad as manager of England Schoolboys. 'I used to watch games in and around Manchester and knew all about him. I knew Steve Kelly, who was in charge of Salford Boys, and he told me of a will-o-the-wisp little boy darting down the wing for Deans.

'When I went to a match at Runcorn on a damp night, I went for a cup of tea at half time and these scouts asked if I knew somebody called Ryan Wilson. I got my little FA diary out and there on the back page, where I used to write down people for England in the future, I had his name, position and his main attributes. I said: "You see, we at England Schoolboys know everything about them. We don't need you scouts!" It was easy with him, though. My granny could tell he would be a star.'

Of course, the teenager had famously been at Manchester City's School of Excellence for over three years, but always harboured dreams of representing the Reds. Posters of United icons Bryan Robson and Mark Hughes adorned his bedroom wall and fellow Welsh winger Mickey Thomas had been his favourite player as a child standing in the Stretford End. 'I knew I was never going to join them,' Giggs later admitted, of his dalliance with the Blues.

Unsurprisingly, the trial spell at The Cliff in late 1986 was an unqualified success for both parties. A hat-trick in a practice match showcased his talents and the starry-eyed teen felt at home. 'I loved the place from day one,' he confessed. 'It was everything I'd hoped it would be.'

As he had also excelled at rugby, and developed a passion for the game after watching his father, there were other options open to a natural sportsman, but his footballing destiny became unstoppable once he hit his teens. Not only did he spend hours on his own with a ball, practising and perfecting his close control, he would also visit other local teams just to train with them and hone his skills.

The manager adopted a hands-on approach usually reserved only for truly extraordinary youngsters and signed Wilson to his first contract on his fourteenth birthday in November 1987, making a personal appearance at the player's house to ensure the paperwork was completed – even though the birthday boy had forgotten about the arranged meeting and returned late to find Ferguson drinking tea with his mother in the family home.

## ... the teenager ... had always harboured dreams of representing the Reds. Posters of United icons Bryan Robson and Mark Hughes adorned his bedroom wall ...

Understandably, much of the new recruit's work with United was undertaken away from prying eyes, as he was carefully nurtured by respected coaches such as Harrison, Kidd and Nobby Stiles. B team manager Kidd, in particular, was a huge influence and even lent a pair of his boots to the prodigy. 'I did but it was nothing out of the ordinary in those days,' confirmed Kidd. 'When I was an apprentice at United, I used to break boots in for the senior players. I remember Denis Law coming back from Italy with some Sivori boots and I actually had a pair of them. But, bloody hell, Ryan could play in anything – even slippers!'

Perhaps the good cop to the harsher figures of Harrison and Ferguson's number two Archie Knox, Kidd was of great assistance and commanded instant respect because of his European Cup-winning exploits. 'One of the greatest things my mum and dad said was: "Remember how we worried about you when you went to United,"' explained the former Reds striker. 'I never thought they did. So what we tried to do – good, bad or indifferent – was to treat the kids like our sons. I just think it is essential to offer that support, care and attention to the boys. For me, Archie doesn't get the credit he deserved. He is one of my best friends in football and I'm indebted to him for the great help he put in with the boys.'

The schoolboy would start to seep into the public's consciousness with his efforts away from his new club. United had a gem on their hands, but would face a battle to temper the hype and expectation surrounding his development into a star because of his exploits elsewhere. 'I remember commentating on him for the first time at Anfield in 1988,' revealed Martin Tyler, who would become a household name with Sky Sports and was behind the microphone when Giggs scored his greatest-ever goal over a decade later. 'Everybody was talking about him. It had happened with a number of players before, Peter Coyne for example, but I wasn't being smart when I told the viewers to watch out for the name. It was pretty well documented. He was already the talk of the town.'

Coyne came through United's ranks in the mid-1970s but ended up forging a career with Crewe Alexandra and Swindon Town, despite scoring against Leicester City in his only start for the Reds. History had shown that big noises at schoolboy level were never guaranteed a smooth rise to superstardom. However, the television coverage of the Granada Cup final, between Salford Boys and Blackburn, somewhat let the genie out of the bottle in Giggs's case. The elegant No. 6 in the green shirt did not score but was involved in all his team's goals in a 3-2 win, motoring through the gears

Even at an early age, silverware was a part of Ryan's career. Here, he joins his United colleagues to celebrate success in the 1989 North West Youth Tournament.

In an early outing at Old Trafford, Ryan continues to build his growing reputation while in action for Salford Boys.

deep into extra time when many of his peers had long since started to flag.

The man of the match opted to star at the home of Liverpool rather than representing United's Under-15s at Old Trafford on the same evening. 'I decided to play for this team instead,' he told the TV cameras from a jubilant dressing room. 'I'd rather play at Anfield because it's a better pitch, really.' Thankfully, this was merely a reference to the terrible state of the surface over at M16 and would give no encouragement to Liverpool's chief scout Ron Yeats, who handed over the trophy in person. 'He looks something special,' confessed Yeats afterwards, little knowing the pain that would be inflicted on a club still very much looking down on United from their lofty perch at the time.

A larger audience would soon be treated to a sight of this exciting prospect, as some of his appearances with England Schoolboys were screened live on ITV. Of course, despite his Welsh roots and desire to represent the country of his birth, the fact he was educated in England meant he was an obvious choice for manager Bushell following the nationwide trials.

'When people ask what was special about him, it was just his innate talent,' explained Bushell. 'Coaches can ruin players' lives, like teachers can ruin kids' lives, because coaches only make a minimal impression on you. It's just a player's innate talent, along with practising to improve and learning things with your head. I used to try to defend against the boys on the training ground when I wanted them to do something. This lad had such a fantastic body swerve, the only reason I ever bumped into him was when I was still being sold the first one and he had come back for his third body swerve because he was that fast!'

An international debut in Northern Ireland followed and proved a baptism of fire off the field, with the Troubles still raging and prompting heightened security for the English visitors. Helicopters

Captain Wilson celebrates victory over Belgium at Wembley with England Schoolboys.

Though Ryan would represent Wales in his senior career, he continued to represent England as a youngster. Here, he's in action against Scotland.

swirled overhead, armed guards were present and sniffer dogs patrolled the dressing room, but the match itself was rather more comfortable and Ryan scored in a 5-0 victory.

Wilson skippered the team for matches against Belgium and West Germany at Wembley and shone in a central midfield role, relishing the increased responsibility, and helped avenge defeat to the Germans a few days later in the Midlands. 'When I made him captain, I told him it was because of his effervescent and extroverted nature,' laughed Bushell. 'I think he jokingly told me to eff off because he never used to speak, only to the lads!'

Giggs scored against Belgium, from the penalty spot, Nick Barmby notched the other goals in a 3-1 win. 'It was a case of give Ryan Wilson the ball and he will do the rest,' said Barmby, a future England international and Premier League stalwart. 'You knew he was going to be brilliant.'

While the outlook may have been rosy for England Schoolboys, the late eighties were a difficult time for Manchester United. Only FA Cup triumphs in 1983 and 1985 had cheered supporters living in the shadow of Liverpool's dominance at home and abroad. Ferguson was certainly under pressure as manager and, having flirted with injecting a batch of youngsters into his team, had settled for an altogether different strategy.

The group, dubbed 'Fergie's Fledglings' in the press, bought the boss some breathing space by catching the fans' imagination and contributing to some inspirational performances, including a rousing 3-1 win against the arch-rivals from Anfield on the first day of 1989. Russell Beardsmore was the chief tormentor on that occasion, and Lee Sharpe, Mark Robins, Lee Martin, David Wilson, Deiniol Graham, Tony Gill and Giuliano Maiorana were others tipped for the top after being given their bows around the same time.

Come the summer and, at the end of another trophyless campaign and 11th spot in the Division One table – one place behind

Millwall – Ferguson adopted a more pragmatic approach to reshaping his side. An unprecedented spending spree saw top English stars Gary Pallister, Neil Webb, Mike Phelan, Danny Wallace and Paul Ince all arrive before the end of September. However, the belief in youth remained instilled in Ferguson and, fortunately for Giggs and the others that followed, he did not abandon his ideals. The influx of a battle-hardened quintet with experience of the division and scope to improve was not going to be a barrier to the progression of the club's brightest prospects.

## 'It was a case of give Ryan the ball and he'll do the rest. You knew he was going to be brilliant.'

**Nick Barmby**
England Schoolboys

'I remember Ferguson saying when he first came in that he wanted a young, vibrant youth system,' said Harrison. 'He insisted: "I'll give them a chance if they're good enough," and he was true to his word. Most of them were local boys as well and the fans absolutely loved them being in the youth team and the first team.'

Giggs was always at the forefront of the Scot's mind – 'the leader of the pack' to use Harrison's phrase – and even the forays into the transfer market failed to divert Ferguson from the task of mirroring the Sir Matt Busby way of promoting from within the ranks.

Promising centre-back Pallister was the most expensive of the acquisitions, and he revealed an early conversation with Ferguson, after joining from Middlesbrough for a club-record fee of £2.3 million. 'I went to watch the youth team with Paul Ince as we were in a hotel and had just signed for the club,' the defender recounted. 'We went to

Old Trafford and sat with the manager. He turned around to me and Incey and said: "There's a kid playing tonight on the left wing called Ryan Wilson and he is going to be a star." I thought: "That's a big statement, gaffer." Here was a spindly-looking 15-year-old kid, but he ran amok against older kids and was terrific.'

Meanwhile, before leaving school, a major change was about to take place for the youngster, albeit one that would have no impact on his career. Ryan decided to adopt his mother's maiden name after his father left home. His parents had never married, and this became apparent when he travelled away with United to youth tournaments in Europe as his passport documentation carried the name on his birth certificate.

In his autobiography, Giggs reveals his embarrassment at this being revealed during a trip to the Blue Stars tournament in Switzerland. 'I'd hated changing in the first place,' he recalled. 'But then I didn't want to change back to Giggs. Kids like stability in their lives and, having got used to one name, the last thing I wanted to do was to start all over again with another. It was all too complicated and drew too much attention for the wrong reasons.'

While the newspapers had initially spoken of a 'new George Best' called Ryan Wilson emerging at Old Trafford, a Sunday tabloid claimed 'the next John Barnes' named Ryan Giggs was on the brink of the first team. It was easy to see why some supporters thought they could be two different players, but he was more concerned that his quality on the pitch was attracting attention, and not worried about the confusion over his name.

His opening forays abroad with United were extremely successful, even allowing for any passport problems. The youth squad returned from Italy with the Grossi Morera trophy in September 1989 to give him a first taste of winning silverware as a United player. Still only fifteen, he was chastised at half time by Harrison, ever the hard taskmaster, for his performance during one of the tournament fixtures, which caused Kidd to question the wisdom of his fellow coach's outburst.

'Make no mistake, I wasn't soft and always told them the truth,' insisted Harrison. 'No lies. The truth hurt sometimes and I hurt a few on the way, but I'd just apologise a few days later and say I was a bit out of order. I felt that was the correct way to do it – tell the truth and then apologise later.'

It may have been unsettling and upsetting, but Ryan featured in every match and a 4-1 victory over Auxerre in the final rounded off a fruitful journey. Trophies must have been in plentiful supply over in Italy as the squad returned with six of them for various feats achieved during the competition, perhaps illustrating, even then, the manner in which silverware appears magnetically drawn to Giggs.

Domestically, he was also making his mark despite his schoolboy status. A Reserves debut in the Pontins League came remarkably early on 23 September, more than two months shy of his 16th birthday, as he replaced Maoirana as a substitute in a 2-1 defeat to Everton. Paul McGuinness, later United's Under-18s manager, and full-back Martin, who would hit the winner eight months later in the FA Cup final replay with Crystal Palace, were also in the team.

It was a rare outing at second-string level for the winger, but he featured in every game during the FA Youth Cup run, a charge that was only halted by Tottenham Hotspur at the semi-final stage. He scored twice at Port Vale, the second of which was a solo effort that started with a run from his own half, and contributed another strike at Burnley in the second round. Despite the disappointment against Spurs, when a 1-0 win in the second leg was insufficient after a two-goal deficit in the capital, he would have another two cracks at lifting the trophy.

His appearance tally reached double figures in the A team, as United won the division, and he mustered seven starts in the Lancashire Division Two for the B side as a gradual introduction to senior football continued over the course of the campaign. Gary Neville remembers being a substitute and watching Giggs score an outstanding goal in an Under-16 friendly against the FA School of Excellence in the November. 'It was an overhead kick that was out of this world,' enthused the defender. 'I couldn't even dream of pulling off a skill like that.'

'He took the mickey out of Viv. Dribbling around him three times and we're all thinking: "Who is this?" He murdered Viv, yet he was a kid and Viv was England's right-back. That was my first memory of Ryan.'

**Steve Bruce**
Manchester United

United won 4-2 with the livewire forward's hat-trick increasing Neville's doubts that he would never possess the quality required to make the grade. 'You were almost embarrassed to turn up at the training ground because you'd think: "Are they all like him?"' Paul Scholes scored the other goal to perhaps exacerbate those fears.

The club also reached the semi-finals of the Saint Brieuc tournament during another overseas sojourn in the following April. Giggs scored against Auxerre and Metz, as well as finding the net in a shoot-out success against Rapid Vienna, a portent of what was to follow on a much greater stage in the Moscow rain of 2008. Meanwhile, as he began training with the first team, so his reputation grew among the elder statesmen at the club. Viv Anderson, a seasoned England international and former European Cup winner, was tormented in direct combat with the fearless rookie and would offer his own sound advice to the upstart.

'You'd expect him to be in awe of all the big players, but nothing fazed him,' explained Anderson. 'He nutmegged me in a training match and, although all the lads thought it was hilarious, I said: "If you ever do that again, you're dead." Or words to that effect!'

Fellow defender Steve Bruce also recalled that incident and the precociousness of a winger with no respect for reputations. 'He took the mickey out of Viv,' he remembered. 'Dribbling around him three times and we're all thinking: "Who is this?" He murdered Viv, yet he was a kid and Viv was England's right-back. That was my first memory of Ryan. Even if I'd wanted to kick him, I couldn't have got near him. I've never seen anyone as natural. He's the only kid at that age you knew would be a superstar. The only one you were entirely sure about.'

Anderson would be the first of many defenders to be given the slip by a wiry winger with boundless confidence and jaw-dropping ability. Plenty of others would learn, in time, that resorting to intimidation or physical threats was futile against such a streetwise individual. Steve Round, who would have a spell as United's assistant manager, met Giggs as Derby County's Reserves right-back and was similarly tormented. 'He gave me an absolutely torrid time,' said Round. 'I couldn't get near him and received the biggest telling off I've ever had in my life afterwards from my manager Arthur Cox, because a schoolboy had run me ragged.'

The season ended well for the club at a senior level. The FA Cup final replay victory over Palace eased the pressure on the manager by bringing the first trophy of his reign and surely proved imperative in ensuring Giggs's career would continue to enjoy a steep upward trajectory. If he had remained at City in 1986, he'd have had five different managers within the ensuing four years. Not only did success at Wembley end speculation over Ferguson's future, it allowed him the opportunity to maintain his vision of building a dynasty at Old Trafford. The fact that Robins and Martin had key roles in the success was another indicator that the conveyor belt was capable of working smoothly at United, despite his early criticisms of the scouting network. These local lads could be trusted to flourish alongside a core of more experienced campaigners. The foundations had been set for future glory.

World Cup fever gripped the country that summer, with Bobby Robson's England reaching the semi-finals in Italy, and the game enjoyed renewed popularity and optimism for the future. There was something similarly exciting enveloping the red half of Manchester as the new term got under way. The United squad that contested the 1990 Milk Cup during the traditional pre-season excursion over the Irish Sea also contained David Beckham, Nicky Butt and Keith Gillespie, as well as Giggs. Despite a 7-1 mauling of local side Maghera Colts, with Giggs scoring and generally running riot, interest in the tournament was ended by Motherwell at the quarter-final stage. Nonetheless, those in Northern Ireland remember the top prospect fondly for his exciting skills.

Four goals for Giggs in the B team in a 6-0 hiding of Carlisle United at the end of September provided mounting evidence that he was outgrowing the youth levels and another quartet of strikes followed in the second round of the FA Youth Cup against Darlington. On his seventeenth birthday, Giggs was handed a five-year contract and it was becoming increasingly clear a first-team call was not far away. The professional status came barely four months after his last deal, as a trainee, and was further indication of the esteem in which he was held by Ferguson and his staff.

'He's never changed,' said youth team coach Harrison. 'He's always been the same – a fabulous player and just a top man.

Alex used to come and watch Ryan in our youth games so I knew he would get his chance young as it's the Manchester United way.'

Harrison explained that, despite occasional pranks from Giggs and his pals Nicky Butt and Scholes, he had no issues with the Welshman. The player agreed to work hard on defending and using his weaker right foot, and it was becoming abundantly clear he was straining at the leash for a bigger platform for his talents.

'I had no run-ins with Ryan,' Harrison insists, despite berating him for that poor performance over in Italy. 'He was one of the quieter ones. He was a sensible lad and we never had a proper run-in. Him and Butty were among the jokers and if somebody's underpants had gone missing in the dressing room, it was always either Giggs or Scholes.'

Another of the youth coaches, Tony Whelan, came to the club in 1990 and remembers why it was deemed unnecessary for the player to learn his trade in the Reserves, as is the conventional route to the first team. On his arrival at the club, the former United and City forward was soon aware of the buzz surrounding the Welsh tyro. 'Ryan was just bursting on to the scene as a youth player and was always very, very talented right from day one,' Whelan stated. 'Everybody was talking about what a good player he was for his age. He was one of the very few players capable of bypassing the Reserves because of his quickness, energy and creativity. He was very hard working as well.'

There was one obvious barrier to his seamless promotion into Manchester United's first-choice left-winger. The current incumbent was Lee Sharpe, still a teenager himself and the recipient of a lucrative contract on the same day that news of Giggs's deal was announced. Rather than emerge through the ranks, the self-assured and chirpy character had been bought from Torquay United and, having initially earned a place in Ferguson's side at left-back, was emerging as an attacking wide player of some repute. Continental defences held no

# Ryan Giggs
## The Man for All Seasons

'Fergie's Fledglings' inspired by home-grown defender Lee Martin, overcome Crystal Palace in the 1990 FA Cup final replay, ensuring success for Alex Ferguson's team shortly before Ryan's emergence on to the senior scene.

**Left:** Success in the FA Youth Cup would arrive in 1992, but Giggs and company would first taste semi-final defeat in 1990 (here, against Tottenham) and 1991.
**Right:** On his 18th birthday, Ryan accepts the keys to his new car from Old Trafford car dealer Jim Quick.

fear for Sharpe, as United embarked on a return to European football, with English sides back from a five-year ban following the Heysel tragedy in Brussels.

Perhaps as a consequence of having Sharpe on the books, Giggs was being groomed as a forward as he pushed ever closer to the first team. The squad was certainly not blessed with a plethora of strikers – Mark Hughes, Brian McClair and Mark Robins were supported by Danny Wallace, who would occasionally switch from his accustomed role on the flanks to a more central position.

'Ryan has got the lot in his locker to be a striker,' Ferguson would declare. 'He penetrates and has lovely balance.' Harrison remains in no doubt to this day that his young charge was more effective down the middle and utilised him in that role with his youth side. 'I thought he was definitely better there,' said the coach. 'I thought he had more room to work. He was brilliant on the wing but better as a striker. Playing centrally, he had a bit more space to run into.'

Christmas came and went with the Reds failing to make a challenge in the title race. Even allowing for his natural modesty, Giggs felt he was not playing particularly well in the A and B teams. However, he was making an impact in the FA Youth Cup, a competition the club has always held in high regard since winning the first five editions with the Busby Babes in the 1950s.

Both Merseyside clubs were vanquished in the early part of 1991 and Giggs scored in the victories away from home on intimidating territory. It did not go unnoticed by Ferguson, who noted his progress with interest and was troubled by the absence of chief attacker Hughes. 'Ryan had a magnificent temperament and a desire to do well,' recalled Kidd. 'People forget, even at an early age, he was feted as one who would make it. So there was more pressure on him because everybody thought he was a stick-on to make the grade. When Alex considered putting him in the first-team squad, I just said: "He's done everything. The boy deserves his chance. The only way we are going

to find out if he is going to do it is by assessing his temperament when he goes in with the seniors and gets his chance." The rest is history.'

A call-up to the squad for the Division One clash at Sheffield United followed in late February. He lost out on a place on the bench to Ferguson's son Darren, another of the club's youngsters deemed ripe for promotion to senior football. The Blades won 2-1 as it became clear that the agonising run without a league title was going to extend into a twenty-fourth year.

After going so close to getting a first taste of top-flight football, the big day arrived in the next fixture – at home to Everton on 2 March 1991. When the Welshman was named as a substitute for the visit of the Toffees, nobody would have expected that he would still be playing for the club over twenty-three years later. Good enough meant old enough, and Giggs was ready to commence a career which would ultimately eclipse all others.

# Most Frequent Opponents

| Opponent | League | | FA Cup | | League Cup | | Champs Lge | | Other | | Total | | Goals |
|----------|--------|-----|--------|-----|------------|-----|------------|-----|-------|-----|-------|------|-------|
| Chelsea | 27 | (6) | 5 | (1) | 3 | | 2 | (1) | 3 | (2) | 40 | (10) | 6 |
| Arsenal | 29 | (9) | 3 | (3) | - | | 0 | (2) | 4 | | 36 | (14) | 2 |
| Liverpool | 34 | (6) | 5 | | 2 | | - | | 1 | | 42 | (6) | 5 |
| Tottenham H | 34 | (4) | 2 | | 1 | (1) | - | | - | | 37 | (5) | 10 |
| Aston Villa | 30 | (4) | 3 | | 2 | | - | | - | | 35 | (4) | 4 |
| Manchester C | 24 | (8) | 3 | | 2 | | - | | - | | 29 | (8) | 4 |
| Blackburn R | 23 | (6) | - | | 5 | | - | | 1 | | 29 | (6) | 2 |
| Newcastle U | 27 | (4) | 1 | (1) | - | | - | | 1 | | 29 | (5) | 5 |
| Everton | 25 | (6) | 0 | (1) | 1 | | - | | - | | 26 | (7) | 8 |
| Middlesbrough | 18 | (5) | 4 | (1) | 3 | | - | | - | | 25 | (6) | 10 |
| Southampton | 21 | (3) | 3 | (2) | - | | - | | - | | 24 | (5) | 7 |
| West Ham U | 20 | (4) | 3 | (1) | 1 | | - | | - | | 24 | (5) | 6 |
| Leeds U | 17 | (3) | 2 | (1) | 2 | | - | | - | | 21 | (4) | 5 |

Most frequent European opponents: 6 (2) games v Bayern Munich, 6 (1) v Juventus, 6 v Deportivo La Coruna, 5 (1) v Real Madrid and 4 (2) v Barcelona

# 2

# Breakthrough Act

Nauseous and shaking, Ryan experienced unfamiliar sensations ahead of the Division One match with Everton that would herald his senior debut as a substitute. He had played at Old Trafford many times before, of course, in a variety of youth matches, yet the magnitude of the occasion caught up with him as he prepared to realise his destiny at such a tender age. The fixture itself could have been deemed one perfect to blood an untested youth product. Howard Kendall's Toffees, a powerhouse in the mid-1980s, were settled in mid-table and smarting from successive defeats. With the European Cup-Winners' Cup run emerging as the priority for United, there was nothing to lose in selecting a raw 17-year-old on the bench.

However, it was an inauspicious start. There would be no dream debut to compare with the ones enjoyed by United players all the way back to Sir Bobby Charlton (who scored two goals on his

first appearance) through to James Wilson, who also netted twice when handed his maiden outing by Giggs, the interim manager, in 2014.

There were still 10 minutes left of the first half when Denis Irwin sustained an injury that meant Giggs's nerves would have to dissipate quickly, as he was thrust into an attacking role alongside the diminutive Danny Wallace. The makeshift strike partnership, while having an abundance of pace, caused no fears for a defence policed by uncompromising old hands Dave Watson and Kevin Ratcliffe. Everton already led through Mike Newell when the substitution was made and, although he was instantly involved when Clayton Blackmore looked for him from two throw-ins, the debutant was largely on the periphery as a poor game unfolded. The dire surface, which he alluded to on that night at Anfield for Salford Boys, contributed to an unattractive spectacle, as sidelined stars Steve Bruce, Bryan Robson and Mark Hughes watched from the stands.

Watson bundled in the second goal and, to add injury to insult, crudely fouled Giggs from behind to leave a cut on his knee, which was the only impression of the occasion he could vividly recall at a later date. He got to his feet and tentatively tugged at his socks, but a few puffs of the cheeks betrayed the pain he was trying to hide from the introductory challenge. 'It doesn't surprise me with Watson,' said Ratcliffe. 'They were all the same with Dave. It was most probably he was slightly quicker than me just to get to Ryan.'

The tackle did no lasting damage, Giggs performed for the Reserves five days later, but there were few positive signs in the overall team performance. Neville Southall had sprung from goal to clear after Giggs raced on to a long ball, while a cross from the left led to Lee Sharpe having a shot saved, but Ferguson's side were poor, showing no signs of the swashbuckling style that would emerge in the coming years. Moreover, despite a crowd of 45,656, the atmosphere was flat. Everton boss Kendall noted he had not heard Old Trafford so quiet

On his arrival in first-team football, Ryan's magnificent balance and poise in possession set him apart.

since playing there in 1972 during a midweek match, rearranged for the afternoon due to power restrictions.

The fans, seeking their own illumination after an insipid performance, were probably aware it would be wise not to judge the boy wonder under such trying circumstances. Ferguson sensibly, and shrewdly, withdrew Giggs from the firing line. A run of seven league matches without a win came to an end with a 4-1 thumping of Luton Town, but others were being preferred in the matchday squad, with Paul Wratten named as substitute on a couple of occasions.

Instead, Giggs spent the rest of March and April with the Reserves and he appeared in 14 Pontins League games in all. On 27 April, he scored in a Lancashire Division One title decider against City, one of seven goals he claimed in 11 games at that level over the course of the season, as a team also containing goalkeeper Mark Bosnich pipped the Blues to top the table by a point.

'Alex knew what he was doing and probably knew before he had that first game that Ryan might struggle a little bit,' said Eric Harrison. 'It was a bit of a taster.' If it was a move aimed at discovering whether the teenager would keep his feet on the ground, it worked. 'Ryan never came and to me and said Alex is not right about this or shouldn't be doing that,' disclosed Harrison. 'Never ever. Not once. There was none of that. The boss did test them because, no question, he was cute like that.'

Out of the blue, on Saturday 4 May, Giggs was reintroduced to the fold and afforded a maiden start at senior level. As fate dictated, it was in the derby against Manchester City – the club he trained with as a schoolboy. Bosnich passed on a rumour of his inclusion around 90 minutes before kick-off, but he initially dismissed it as a wind-up.

When Ferguson delivered the words: 'Ryan, you play on the left,' Giggs was stunned but mentally prepared. It took only 22 minutes to make his mark, although his winning goal should really have been debited to Colin Hendry. The full debutant may have got the faintest touch to Brian McClair's cross, but it hit the sliding City centre-back and crept past Martyn Margetson. Club statistician Cliff Butler concedes it should be recorded as an own goal, but Hendry told reporters afterwards to 'give it to the young boy' and, in the days before the dubious goals panel, the record books continue to show Giggs enjoyed a scoring first start and he was keen to stress it did hit his foot before Hendry's intervention.

There were other moments to cherish from somebody described as 'a little spindly-legged' and 'not quite having the pace of Sharpe but rather more control' in the match reports compiled for the following day's newspapers. The *Independent* noted one run had full-back Andy Hill 'going in three directions at once'.

Mal Donaghy, the oldest of all Giggs's United teammates, replaced him with 11 minutes remaining to allow the youngster a warm ovation on a day to remember when felt he performed well. 'When he first came into the team, he was a flying machine,' said Donaghy. 'In those days you could tackle, but I saw defenders try to hack him down and he was just too quick for them.'

For all the pleasure extracted from emerging victorious in the derby, City still finished above the Reds in the Division One table. Nonetheless, there was a glorious finale to the campaign on the horizon, when a 2-1 victory over Barcelona secured the club's second European trophy triumph, with Mark Hughes scoring both goals against his former club in a riotously jubilant Rotterdam.

Giggs was present at De Kuip but did not feel worthy of playing a prominent part in the celebrations, having failed to be involved in a single minute of the European Cup-Winners' Cup run. Classified as a foreigner by the UEFA rules then in place, he would have to wait for his chance and, in any case, Sharpe was still terrorising full-backs with his blistering pace on the left flank and was very much a key figure for Ferguson. The youngster still soaked up the atmosphere and savoured the elation only trophy winning can provide. It was something he

▼
Ryan steals in to score his first senior goal for the club, with a little help from Manchester City defender Colin Hendry.

would have to get used to. 'It would have been a good experience and I suppose something to dream about and hopefully attain when he got his opportunity,' opined McClair. 'Ryan has always taken his opportunities.'

There was a mood of delirium on the terraces and a growing belief that Ferguson was turning things around at the club, as the club had also reached the League Cup final that season. If the FA Cup win in 1990 bought him more time, success at European level – as rank underdogs against Johan Cruyff's Barcelona 'Dream Team', no less – was a natural springboard to a sustained tilt at the much-coveted league title.

If exciting times beckoned for the club, there was still a natural air of caution surrounding the latest prodigy in the public consciousness. Comparisons with the iconic George Best were inevitable and unavoidable, but the footballing world had seen it all before and appeared a little weary at the trumpeting of this latest pretender.

At Old Trafford, many had been shouldered with the tag of the 'new Best', from Willie Morgan through to Sammy McIlroy and Norman Whiteside. The latter was the last 17-year-old to graduate to the professional ranks ahead of schedule at the club and, after being the youngest player ever to appear at the World Cup finals in 1982, his career was virtually over by now, wrecked by injury at the age of twenty-six. It was another reminder that nothing can be taken for granted, no matter how promising a player can appear in his late teens, and Giggs would play in Whiteside's testimonial in the following May.

Ferguson, always a fatherly influence to his young star, would throw a protective blanket around the latest prodigy. There was a press blackout and he was gagged from speaking to those eager to know more about his life and personality. 'This club is a refuge for Ryan,' explained the manager. 'He can come here and be sheltered by us.' The media ban helped, as the player acknowledged despite growing a little frustrated with it over time, and it was widely acknowledged as another shrewd move by the manager.

'It was difficult to keep a lid on things in a sense,' confessed Ferguson. 'But not in terms of the person we're talking about, because he would come to me if he had any issues with the press and I would deal with it. Ryan came into the team at a time when there were still remnants of the great George Best, and every young winger that came to United was the new George, and Ryan had to live with that expectation.

'He wasn't the next George Best, though; he was the new Ryan Giggs. He was his own man. For our part, we dealt with it well and I was delighted with how the staff all dealt with it. We had the experience, through Matt's experience with George Best, of how to deal with young players in terms of success and how they lived their lives, and that was really important.'

It appeared as though the patient approach was continuing to be adopted by Ferguson when the 1991-92 pre-season campaign started in earnest. Rather than link up with the first team, Giggs embarked on a tour to Cornwall with the Reserves, scoring in a win against Liverpool but losing to Plymouth Argyle, before also finding the net during a competition in Hilversum in the Netherlands.

However, Lee Sharpe had started what became a persistent battle with injuries and illness, with a hernia problem causing particular concern. The 20-year-old did not resurface until the final throes of that year, making his comeback on 29 December against Leeds United, the club he would later join. The absence of the left-winger prompted Ferguson to elevate Giggs into his squad, and he was named on the bench for the opening game of the season against Notts County at an expectant Old Trafford. With the squad bolstered by the arrival of goalkeeper Peter Schmeichel, full-back Paul Parker and winger Andrei Kanchelskis, hopes were high that a sustained challenge would be mounted for the elusive title.

Parker was instantly impressed by his new colleague, after moving north from Queens Park Rangers, and realised why the manager had included this rookie 'with a short body but legs that were never-ending'. 'I fancied myself against everybody, but I didn't want to go anywhere near him,' confessed the England international. 'The thing about Ryan was he had that arrogance, but a good kind of arrogance. He knew how good he was and how quick he was. He always believed he could outrun you. In the short sprints, he would start running and then flip around and keep going backwards as you're chasing him. He would spin to look around at you and spin off again. He was a Speedy Gonzalez. You don't often get someone that quick who is just as good as a long-distance runner.'

The early signs for the new-look team were extremely promising. Schmeichel kept four successive clean sheets and Giggs remained heavily involved, starting in the third game at Everton and meeting familiar foes Watson and Ratcliffe again in a goalless stalemate. Ratcliffe again noted his countryman's potential: 'He was the first one I'd seen where you could say, without any doubt, that he was going to be a player. It's a similar feeling to when you hear a song for the first time and know it's going to be a number one hit.'

Giggs felt the match where he genuinely came of age was against Norwich City at Old Trafford on 7 September. The crestfallen Canaries were demolished by three goals inside eight first-half minutes, with the winger scoring the third from an extremely unforgiving angle and also hitting the woodwork in an eye-catching display. 'He is going to become a hell of a player,' anticipated Hughes after the game. 'He doesn't have the physical power yet but that will come in the next year or two.' The response to this prediction in one broadsheet was for the writer – who shall remain unnamed and unshamed – to curiously ponder: 'The question is whether Giggs will last a year or two.' At least this was one way of keeping his feet on the ground after such a stellar showing.

On the day of Ryan's first outstanding United performance, Norwich City were run ragged at Old Trafford. Ian Crook tries to halt his progress on this occasion.

The United faithful were starting to appreciate what the hype was all about, and Giggs destroyed Cambridge United in the League Cup. A week later, he became Wales' youngest-ever international when appearing for the last six minutes of a 4-1 defeat to West Germany in Nuremberg. Thankfully for Ferguson, he was able to enlist familiar minders to protect his protégé over the course of the trip.

'We were all laughing at his skinny legs,' recalled Red Star's Marino Pusic, who was among the travelling party. 'Then he went on the pitch and got the ball. We stopped laughing.'

**Marino Pusic**
Red Star Belgrade

'Most probably, the worst thing for Ferguson was Ryan going away with the Welsh squad, as I remember the hype around him at the time was massive,' explained Ratcliffe. 'He was well looked after by Clayton Blackmore and Hughes. I'm sure they were warned by Alex to keep him away from the lads who would go for a drink. He was never really out of their reach. As a young kid coming away, he had all these gadgets, including a Nintendo Game Boy with Tetris – it was state-of-the-art back then! The people around him were more interested in the computer he had than Ryan Giggs the player.'

Back home, the Reds were flying but fresh lessons were just around the corner. Atlético Madrid ended United's reign as European Cup-Winners' Cup-holders in emphatic fashion (winning 3-1 on aggregate) and Giggs found it difficult in the face of some cynical continental marking in the second leg. It was clear he would need to become a quick learner and the signs were positive in that respect.

Soon afterwards, he won his first senior trophy at the club as Red Star Belgrade were beaten 1-0 in the European Super Cup. The tie was played over one leg at Old Trafford, due to the conflict in the former Yugoslavia, and the Reds were fortunate, despite having a Steve Bruce penalty saved, as Dejan Savicevic sparkled for the visitors. Although Giggs must have marvelled at the Montenegrin magician, he impressed when coming off the bench for Lee Martin, after McClair converted the winner when Neil Webb's strike rebounded off the woodwork. 'We were all laughing at his skinny legs,' recalled Red Star's Marino Pusic, who was among the travelling party. 'Then he went on the pitch and got the ball. We stopped laughing.'

It was, nonetheless, a reminder of the harsh nature of this man's game for a callow youth not long out of school. Even ignoring the opposition awaiting on the pitch, integration into a dressing room stocked with some huge personalities was a daunting prospect. Giggs still spent much of his time with his own age group instead, and later admitted feeling uncomfortable mixing with his senior colleagues, saying: 'I was intimidated by the older players and their sarcasm.'

Giggs's bemusement at some of the banter included admitting McClair's jokes and dry wit would often go right over his head. 'He still doesn't understand my sense of humour,' insisted the Scot. 'I take that as a massive pat on the back! Look, we never made it difficult for anybody. It was a good dressing room and a great bunch of people there to help him both on and off the pitch.'

As he was still eligible for the FA Youth Cup, it was understandable that he would spend a lot of time with friends such as Paul Scholes, Nicky Butt, George Switzer, Gary Neville and John O'Kane. There was still a personal desire to lift the famous trophy with his closest allies. 'Ryan would only come into our dressing room at The Cliff when the gaffer called a meeting,' explained Parker. 'He wasn't

in it for more than a few minutes. In my time, he didn't really go in the first-team one on the left-hand side; he'd be with the Reserves in the second one. He stuck with them and was very close to them. Ryan never forgot where he came from and that tells you everything about him.'

Ferguson was certainly grateful when assistance was provided by the experienced professionals, who would soon realise the new kid on the block was in the team on merit and could play a key role in attaining any future success. 'All those old ones were very important to Ryan,' said the boss. 'Steve Bruce, Bryan Robson, McClair and Hughes in particular. There was a great story when the players wound him up and told him that he was due a club car. So he came up to me and asked about getting one. I said: "Club car? You'll be lucky to get a f****** bike!" The other players were waiting outside my office for him and, my word, they gave him some stick. They wound him right up for falling into their trap. But the older players were great to him, as they were with all the young players. Paul Ince was also big influence on Ryan; they were very close together. So they all played a part in his career.'

With the integration growing easier, magical performances gradually became the norm and those present realised their good fortune at witnessing such a burgeoning talent. He leaped to volley in a McClair cross against West Ham United and dribbled around goalkeeper Jon Hallworth in style during a 6-3 Boxing Day extravaganza at Oldham Athletic. A display at Crystal Palace had the London press purring, but three perilous excursions over the Pennines to face Leeds United, the most hostile of rivals, would test the mettle of the willowy Welshman.

Remarkably, United landed trips to Elland Road in both domestic cup competitions to coincide with a league visit to West Yorkshire. The Reds had triumphed in a stormy League Cup semi-final over two legs a year earlier, only to lose to Sheffield Wednesday in the final, but

Atletico Madrid provided a tough first lesson in the art of continental marking and tackling in the European Cup Winners' Cup.

As Giggs's reputation builds, so too do the demands on his time – such as this Old Trafford photo shoot to promote scratchcards.

top-of-the-table Leeds were clear title rivals and the trio of matches either side of New Year would be a major examination of character and resolve.

United won both cup ties, 3-1 in the Rumbelows Cup (with Giggs sliding in to add the third goal in front of the away support), and 1-0 in the FA Cup, as Hughes hit the winner against the run of play. Yet, crucially, the league contest ended in a 1-1 draw and the extra cup fixtures ultimately counted against Ferguson's men during an arduous run-in.

Giggs certainly proved his ice-cool temperament in the bear-pit atmosphere at Elland Road. In one glorious movement, he robbed ex-Red Gordon Strachan and then avoided David Batty's exuberant challenge with a delicious rollback. It was a matador moment that encapsulated his confidence and bravery in beating aggressors with sheer skill and bedevilment.

Hence, the comparisons with the iconic Best grew, as the Northern Irishman had made a habit of teasing hatchet men with designs on physical confrontation. Another legend, Denis Law, was asked for his opinion on the debate and provided the most perceptive of answers. Law: 'Ryan is good but George, even at that age, was an exceptional player,' the club's legendary marksman explained. 'But when you consider how Ryan coped with those three games at Elland Road, you begin to recognise the lad's enormous strength of character and here may lie his special ingredient.'

In February, United became the first top-flight team to be knocked out of the FA Cup in a penalty shoot-out after a 2-2 draw in the replay with Alan Shearer's Southampton. Giggs had the nerve to take one himself, memorably juggling the ball as he advanced to the spot, but fired too close to Tim Flowers. It was a bitter blow for the youngster, who had seen a penalty saved for England Schoolboys against West Germany but never missed again from 12 yards for United.

It was left to the League Cup to provide a route to Wembley and an extra-time winner in the semi-final against Middlesbrough, shinning in a volley at the Stretford End, proved Giggs was capable of not only emphasising his remarkable stamina but was able to make match-winning contributions at crucial stages of key games. The home fans rejoiced but, unfortunately, United's league title bid faltered.

The Reds endured three outings without a goal until Giggs, wearing the No. 7 shirt, cut inside from the right past Neil Pointon to beat Tony Coton in another Manchester derby. Although he was developing a knack for upsetting the club's neighbours – he was, after all, feared by the Blues and loved by the Reds, as the supporters sang – Keith Curle's penalty earned a point.

## 'Ryan produces all sorts of wonderful things that people don't dare to try on the training ground, let alone the pitch.'

**Brian McClair**
Manchester United

Away from the tension associated with bidding to end the title drought, the League Cup was secured for the first time in the club's history. Giggs conducted a rare television interview beforehand, flanked by his protective manager, and was determined to savour the occasion. He did just that, returning a touch from McClair into the striker's path for the only goal against Nottingham Forest. 'Ryan produces all sort of wonderful things that people don't dare to try on the training ground, let alone the pitch,' commented the goalscorer. 'It's wonderful to be winning things. Ryan had been around games

like the FA Cup final replay at Wembley and it's something you always want to be involved in yourself.'

Facing a fixture pile-up of damaging proportions, there would be no third major trophy in Giggs's first full season as the one most desperately cherished continued to elude the Reds. Between 18 and 22 April, United drew with Luton Town and lost to both Forest, who exacted some revenge for Wembley, and a West Ham side that ultimately finished bottom of the table. There was also a well-documented brush with Ferguson that cost Giggs a month's wages when he and Sharpe enjoyed a night out in Blackpool after the Forest defeat.

The manager stormed into Sharpe's house and, sensing another party atmosphere with several members of both sexes present, his volcanic temper erupted towards the youthful pair, causing Giggs to feel he had been, in his words, 'monstered'. Tellingly, the threat used by the boss was to call Ryan's mother, which perhaps not only illustrates how young he still was but also the influence she retained over the budding superstar.

As United ran out of steam, Leeds drew inspiration from the influence provided by recent acquisition Eric Cantona. The final dagger through the heart was provided by Liverpool on the last Sunday in April, soon after a fortunate win for Leeds at Sheffield United. Anfield crowed and mocked in unison as the hosts won 2-0, even Ian Rush scored against his bogey side, and it was the most excruciating of afternoons for everybody associated with the club. None more so than for Giggs, who obliged when asked for an autograph as he trudged away from the ground, only for the Liverpool fan in question to rip it up in his face.

Yet Ferguson's teams would be characterised by growing stronger in adversity and using such dejection to fuel the desire for redemption or success. The manager told Giggs to remember the incident with the supporter and draw on the experience. 'I was sat in the dressing room as an eighteen-year-old watching grown men cry,'

Giggs pressures Arsenal defender Colin Pates during a hard-fought draw with George Graham's reigning champions at Old Trafford.

The Rumbelows League Cup winners milk the moment at Wembley after overcoming Nottingham Forest, courtesy of a Brian McClair winner assisted by Ryan.

revealed Giggs in 2014. 'I saw then how much football and winning meant to people. How much it meant to professionals.'

The PFA Young Player of the Year was one consolation prize, beating Shearer to the award, and he seemed to take some pleasure in Pallister being far more nervous about giving his speech as the main winner. The FA Youth Cup also eased some of the pain as he started the second leg against Crystal Palace and lifted the trophy as skipper following a 6-3 aggregate triumph. Double strikes against Tranmere Rovers and Tottenham in earlier rounds had certainly earned him the right to return to the line-up at Old Trafford, three days after shining and helping to lift the mood in the final game of the first-team season against Spurs. Coach Harrison had to disappoint one player – Robbie Savage. 'Poor Robbie,' said the coach. 'What a crazy man but a super lad, and I had to leave him out to bring Ryan in. He wasn't too happy but I said: "That's football. It's one of those things."' Giggs certainly enjoyed the thrill of spearheading the Class of '92. 'At the time, there was nothing better,' he recalled.

That said, losing out to Leeds in the last-ever season before the launch of the Premier League hurt deeply. Recovering from such a setback would be a colossal challenge, even for a renowned motivator like Ferguson. In truth, the title had never seemed so close and yet so utterly elusive. Was there genuinely a jinx, as the manager himself had referred to in his early days at the club?

The Premier League ushered in a new era for English football, with Sky TV's screening of a wide array of the following term's games soon to bring fortunes for the players and make them all household names. United would always be a major attraction but started terribly. Brian Deane plundered the very first goal of the new division, as Sheffield United won the opener and a 3-0 home loss to Everton set alarm bells ringing. Form improved and Giggs got off the mark before August was out with a rare header at Forest. A classic strike was supplied a month later when he notched an incredible

Giggs accelerates through a gap left by Michael Thomas and Rob Jones, but cannot help United avoid defeat at Anfield on his darkest day in football.

Sir Matt Busby presents awards to Ryan and Jason Lydiate, named Jimmy Murphy Young Player of the Year and Denzil Haroun Reserve Team Player of the Year respectively.

'A footballer of his calibre pops up maybe once in a couple of generations. He's a defender's worst nightmare. It's chilling the way Ryan seems to float over the surface rather than run like the rest of us ... He is so quick and checks with that instant stop ... markers just can't live with him.'

solo goal at Tottenham, knocking the ball impudently through Jason Cundy's legs and skipping past Ian Walker before lashing into the inviting net.

'His ability is Heaven sent,' gushed Ferguson. 'A footballer of his calibre pops up maybe once in a couple of generations. He's a defender's worst nightmare. It's chilling the way Ryan seems to float over the surface rather than run like the rest of us. So light on his feet and blessed with wonderful, wonderful balance. I can't stress that quality too much. He is so quick and checks with that instant stop that makes you think he was born with an ABS braking system in his feet. Whatever the secret, markers just can't live with him. They are falling all over the place and he is still on his feet ready for the next one.'

However, the side struggled again, particularly in front of goal, so Ferguson pulled off a masterstroke in the improbable signing of Cantona from Leeds, and fortunes were almost instantly transformed. Giggs, and his teammates, enjoyed playing with the talismanic Frenchman and everything clicked into place. Ryan spun in a sublime

**Alex Ferguson**
Manchester United

Reds skipper Ryan and Crystal Palace counterpart Mark Holman exchange pennants ahead of the 1992 FA Youth Cup final decider.

Norwich again suffer at Giggs's feet, as the high-flying Canaries are blown apart at Carrow Road as the swashbuckling visitors close in on the Premier League title.

shot against Coventry City as the year ended and bagged a beauty at QPR, running through the defence to lob over Tony Roberts.

A free-kick accounted for Brighton & Hove Albion in the FA Cup fourth round and he hit a real purple patch in February, scoring four times in three matches, including two inside a minute, to prompt an amazing turnaround against Southampton and old adversary Flowers. 'Speaking as a fan, I think he's pure magic,' conceded the Saints keeper magnanimously. 'He comes down the pitch like a snake, side-winding all the way.'

When United travelled to East Anglia to face Norwich in early April, there was certainly plenty of venom in the attack as the Canaries, title contenders themselves, were blitzed inside 21 minutes by a breathtaking display of pace and power. Giggs was very much to the fore, opening the scoring in the thrilling 3-1 victory, and the belief grew that this could finally be the year to bring home the championship. When Bruce popped up with two late headers against Sheffield Wednesday, it put the Reds in the driving seat and the title triumph was confirmed ahead of Blackburn's visit to Manchester, when Ron Atkinson's Aston Villa suffered a shock loss to Oldham.

The players enjoyed an impromptu celebration at Bruce's house on the eve of the game, but still lifted themselves on an emotional night in front of the watching Sir Matt Busby. Giggs grabbed the equaliser with a superb free-kick and inspired a fine comeback to bring the house down with a 3-1 win.

'Giggs has the ball at his feet and the world at his feet,' commentated Sky's Martin Tyler at a euphoric Old Trafford. 'He certainly did back then and he certainly didn't disappoint either,' the commentator would later stress at the end of the player's career.

Even allowing for the garish jackets Giggs and his friend Ince sported afterwards, it was his talent on the field that was attracting all the attention and placing him firmly in the spotlight. The winger

Do not adjust your sets – Paul Ince and his close pal show off garish jackets as United's championship drought is ended in questionable style.

even broke his silence to give a short press conference and enthused: 'When my goal went in, it got the party going again! The atmosphere was brilliant – I don't think I'll ever witness anything quite like it again.' Little did he realise, this was still just the very beginning.

# Season-by-Season Appearance Career Record

| Season | League | FA Cup | League Cup | Champs Lge | Other Eur | Other | Total |
|---|---|---|---|---|---|---|---|
| 1990-91 | 1 (1) | 1 | • | • | • | • | 1 (1) |
| 1991-92 | 32 (6) | 2 (1) | 6 (2) | • | 1 | 0 (1) | 41 (9) |
| 1992-93 | 40 (1) | 2 | 2 | • | 1 | • | 45 (1) |
| 1993-94 | 32 (6) | 7 | 6 (2) | 4 | • | 1 | 50 (8) |
| 1994-95 | 29 | 6 (1) | • | 3 | • | 1 | 39 (1) |
| 1995-96 | 30 (3) | 7 | 2 | • | 2 | • | 41 (3) |
| 1996-97 | 25 (1) | 3 | • | 6 (1) | • | 1 | 35 (2) |
| 1997-98 | 28 (1) | 2 | • | 5 | • | 1 | 36 (1) |
| 1998-99 | 20 (4) | 5 (1) | 1 | 9 | • | 1 | 36 (5) |
| 1999-00 | 30 | • | • | 11 | • | 3 | 44 |
| 2000-01 | 24 (7) | 2 | • | 9 (2) | • | 1 | 36 (9) |
| 2001-02 | 18 (7) | 0 (1) | • | 13 | • | 1 | 32 (8) |
| 2002-03 | 32 (4) | 3 | 4 (1) | 13 (2) | • | • | 52 (7) |
| 2003-04 | 29 (4) | 5 | • | 8 | • | 1 | 43 (4) |
| 2004-05 | 26 (6) | 2 (2) | 1 | 6 | • | 1 | 36 (8) |
| 2005-06 | 22 (5) | 1 (1) | 3 | 4 (1) | • | • | 30 (7) |
| 2006-07 | 25 (5) | 6 | • | 8 | • | • | 39 (5) |
| 2007-08 | 26 (5) | 2 | • | 4 (5) | • | 1 | 33 (10) |
| 2008-09 | 15 (13) | 2 | 3 (1) | 6 (5) | • | 2 | 28 (19) |
| 2009-10 | 20 (5) | 0 (1) | 2 | 1 (2) | • | 0 (1) | 23 (9) |
| 2010-11 | 19 (6) | 1 (2) | 1 | 6 (2) | • | 0 (1) | 27 (11) |
| 2011-12 | 14 (11) | 2 | 1 | 3 | 2 | • | 22 (11) |
| 2012-13 | 12 (10) | 2 (2) | 1 | 3 (2) | • | • | 18 (14) |
| 2013-14 | 6 (6) | • | 2 | 6 (1) | • | 1 | 15 (7) |
| Totals | 555 (117) | 62 (12) | 35 (6) | 128 (23) | 6 | 16 (3) | 802 (161) |

**Other:** Charity/Community Shield 12 (2); European Super Cup 0 (1); Club World Cup 1; Club World Championship 2; Inter-Continental Cup 1.

# 3

# A Roller Coaster Ride

'I was determined not to be a one-season wonder and worked very hard on my game in pre-season.' For a teenager fresh from winning his first league title, Ryan's attitude must have been music to the ears of his manager Alex Ferguson, himself never one to dwell on past achievements.

Giggs was the first footballer ever to be named the PFA Young Player of the Year twice, after earning the acclaim of his peers again in 1993 to retain the award. The hype was starting to get a little out of control, as those initially somewhat wary of making firm predictions reassessed their views in light of his clear success at both personal and club level. Warnings were still being delivered by some fearing the worst, as Premier League footballers began to achieve unimaginable riches, enough to turn anybody's head and dampen their desire for the less glamorous aspects of the game.

# Ryan Giggs
## The Man for All Seasons

'Giggs will soon lose his football virginity and face the enormity of his potential,' pundit Garth Crooks eloquently wrote in one newspaper column. 'Whether he remains in control of the magic exuded by Manchester United, or destroyed by it, will ultimately depend on him.'

Crooks had first-hand experience of Old Trafford and its all-consuming nature as a loan signing during Ron Atkinson's reign. The striker's teammates had been suffocated by the expectation and haunted by the glorious ghosts of the past. One of the most revered of those icons of the Sir Matt Busby era, the legendary George Best, was actively being encouraged to contribute to magazine features and television documentaries alongside the boy with the Midas touch.

'I've heard so many times about young players who are going to be great,' said the Northern Irishman. 'He's not only fulfilled it but he's getting better. I hate all that stuff about comparisons, but I hope he takes it as a compliment. I certainly do. I think he's the best in the world at the moment. In a few years' time, they will start saying a player will be the "new Ryan Giggs", as I think he will become that great.'

The modest, respectful youngster offered his own views during the lengthy discussions, but pointed out he had Ferguson to steer him away from the pitfalls that had consumed Best and was remaining admirably level-headed. 'I wouldn't mind being half the player George was,' he conceded. 'I would be a star.'

Meanwhile, Ferguson made only one addition to his championship-winning squad, fighting off fierce competition from Blackburn Rovers to land Nottingham Forest's much-coveted midfielder Roy Keane. The Irishman respected his new colleague as he quickly settled in at Old Trafford. 'Ryan was light years ahead of me in terms of ability and maturity,' Keane later insisted. 'He is funny, cheeky and blessed with extraordinary talent.'

Before the memorable 1993-94 season started, there was a tour of South Africa which allowed Giggs to meet Nelson Mandela,

**Left:** The new Best? The oft-compared duo of George and Ryan pose together at the 1993 PFA Awards, where the Welshman retained his Young Player of the Year gong.
**Right:** Another famous face accompanies Giggs as he meets South African president Nelson Mandela.

Ryan thrills the football followers in South Africa with his ball-juggling skills.

as he was selected to head up to the VIP box with Ferguson, even though he was not actually playing against Kaizer Chiefs. The reason for the request was simple – he was one of the president's favourite players.

That came after the second fixture of the trip. The first, a friendly with Arsenal at Ellis Park, was a misnomer as Bryan Robson was sent off. The animosity extended off the field after the match, with Clayton Blackmore revealing: 'The lads were going out for a drink, so the youngsters came along as well. I had the bouncer's job and we bumped into the Arsenal lads. They were a bit drunk and trying to get to Ryan, talking about George Best and attempting to get him drinking. I just made sure I got him out of the club. We went for a nice, quiet drink somewhere else. It was a good job as, a bit later on, the rest of our lads nearly started fighting with the Arsenal guys because they were pulling faces behind Roy Keane's back and Robbo stepped in.'

# The Frenchman was orchestrating an enchanting brand of flowing football and regularly combining almost telepathically with the lightning-quick Welshman.

The two factions would soon resume their rivalry in a more conventional on-field setting but, as Giggs had been substituted for Robson, he missed out on taking a penalty against the Gunners in a Charity Shield shoot-out victory at Wembley. He wouldn't wait long to find the net though, sweeping home the first goal of the Reds' Premier League title defence in the season opener at Norwich City.

Robson also scored in that victory and, while the capture of Keane, the form of Ince and the passage of time were conspiring to reduce his influence on the field, the former England captain was a hugely important figure in Giggs's early years, providing unyielding protection – to the point that he would swap positions with his young cohort if a full-back dished out a few unwelcome verbal threats.

'When I came through the ranks at West Brom, I was the only young player but the experienced lads always looked after me and gave me good information about what to do,' he asserted. 'I took that on board and, because people looked after me, I wanted to give advice to the likes of Ryan and Lee Sharpe when they came through, to help them go on and become top players.'

Both zestful wingers were having a major impact, adding silk down the flanks to complement the steel and aggression regularly provided by the warriors in the spine of the side. Giggs flighted a glorious free-kick past Newcastle United's Pavel Srnicek in a 1-1 draw before Sharpe hit a double at Aston Villa and netted in the next two league outings as well.

United were a force to be reckoned with and it was difficult to envisage any problems on the horizon when Giggs finished off a flowing move at Sheffield Wednesday by converting an Eric Cantona through ball. The Frenchman was orchestrating an enchanting brand of flowing football and regularly combining almost telepathically with the lightning-quick Welshman. Thankfully, Giggs signed another lucrative contract to quash rumours of a possible to move to Italy, with both Milan clubs alerted by a comment he made in his first in-depth interview when he claimed he would like to play in Serie A at some stage of his career. Inter Milan would continue to pursue him through until his thirties.

'Ryan shouldn't be thinking about moving abroad,' United chairman Martin Edwards had advised in the previous May. 'If good players are prepared to commit their whole careers to us, we are ready

▼
Despite Giggs's efforts, United's first tilt at the European Cup since 1969 is ended by Galatasaray in the Ali Sami Yen cauldron.

to make similar arrangements but, if a player wants to go, no club in the world is powerful enough to keep him.' The quote filled every United fan with a little dread. It is reasonable to suggest the general feeling was any move could be postponed for several years, but £15 million or the billions of lira that represented would not be easily dismissed.

At least that was something to worry about further down the line. On the pitch, collective complacency certainly crept in against Galatasaray. Two goals ahead inside 13 minutes, it took an 81st-minute equaliser by Cantona to preserve a proud unbeaten home record in Europe, but the most frustrating of second leg stalemates at the hostile Ali Sami Yen Stadium sent this all-conquering team spinning out of the Champions League at the second hurdle. If Elland Road had provided a white-hot experience during domestic duties, this was a furnace worthy of the 'Hell' moniker supplied by the fanatical supporters.

It was a torturous experience for the entire squad. Cantona was sent off and the players were attacked by riot police as they made their way down the steps towards the dressing room. Future excursions to Leeds would seem far less perilous in comparison. Yet for all the heat raining down from the terraces, Giggs had gone off the boil. Still adapting to European football, he had performed poorly against the Turkish side and was, after all, occupying one of the precious 'foreigner' slots due to his Welsh nationality (at the time, UEFA rules allowed British clubs to field no more than two foreign players, along with three British and Irish players).

Ferguson decided to start him on the bench, as he had done at Everton in late October, four days later at Maine Road for another Manchester derby – one that would go down in history as a genuine classic. When he entered the fray, possibly with a point to prove, United trailed 2-1, with Cantona's goal, pouncing on a Michel Vonk error, having already halved the arrears. It seemed Giggs's game was largely dependent on his athleticism at this time – pace, stamina and that remarkable balance. His very first touch questioned this notion. It was beautifully simple, incisive and intelligent; an instant pass to the back post that ripped the heart out of the City defence and Cantona gleefully plundered an equaliser. Not content with a point, Keane stole in at the back post to convert a Denis Irwin cross and the comeback was complete.

Soon afterwards, there was anguish on the international front when Paul Bodin crashed a penalty against the bar and Wales missed out on a World Cup finals berth by losing to Romania. By now, Giggs had proved a dazzling addition to his country's ranks, tormenting Belgium and scoring a free-kick earlier in the year, but it was to be familiar tale of disappointment throughout his Welsh career. At least he dispelled one myth about his international allegiance: 'I went to school in England but, because my parents are Welsh, I simply couldn't have played for England,' he stated, as left-wing became a problem position for the English.

Hughes and Blackmore would provide support, but Wales were always to fall short of realising Giggs's dream of playing in a major international tournament. He would also be subjected to special attention by those out to nullify the small nation's obvious threat. Blackmore explained: 'I especially used to look after him with Wales and, if someone had a dig, we'd give the guy a dig back. We used to say: "If you touch Ryan, you're going to get it back," but it used to go on in those days. He was such an important player for us.'

At club level, the goals continued to come thick and fast, including a brace at Oldham Athletic, with enough regularity to provoke the introduction of a new, nonchalant celebration apparently devoid of emotion. A simple whirl of a finger passed for acknowledgement of his achievement to the supporters, although he could still be coerced into a choreographed dance with Paul Ince when collared by his best friend.

But Giggs was also adopting a more serious approach to his game, unsettled by the first criticisms of his contribution. 'I know I've still got a lot to learn,' he stressed. 'The manager is always pointing things out to me that I should or shouldn't be doing and I don't feel happy with myself unless I'm learning something new at every training session.'

## 'He has such a wonderful attitude. At the moment he reminds me of a lad who knows all the card tricks but has still to learn how to play cards.'

**Alex Ferguson**
Manchester United

Ferguson acknowledged the poster boy of British football was not the finished article, even if he remained bewitched by his potential and encouraged by his mental strength. 'He has such a wonderful attitude,' declared the manager. 'At the moment, he reminds me of a lad who knows all those card tricks but has still to learn how to play cards.'

The genius could not be suppressed for long. A glorious chip over Bruce Grobbelaar at Anfield was sheer impudence and a run at Loftus Road left the Queens Park Rangers defenders trailing in his wake like a string of Keystone Kops. 'The boy's a genius – it could almost be George Best,' enthused commentator Clive Tyldesley, illustrating why the comparisons would continue.

Sandwiching those games were two 1-0 victories, one at Tottenham and the other at home to Everton. The latter was hugely significant because it fell just two days after the death of club president Sir Matt Busby at the age of eighty-four. It seemed an entirely fitting tribute that Giggs would score the only goal of a landmark occasion

Ryan pounces to score against Oldham in December 1993, just beating Roy Keane to the punch.

A wonderful chip flies past Mark Wright on course to clearing Liverpool goalkeeper Bruce Grobbelaar in a thrilling 3-3 draw at Anfield.

and provide flashes of joyful, unfettered inspiration that evoked memories of the Busby Babes themselves.

Giggs also opened the scoring against Sheffield Wednesday and Oldham, but United had to overcome a tricky period when Cantona collected red cards in successive games and Alan Shearer inspired title rivals Blackburn to a 2-0 triumph when the teams went head-to-head at Ewood Park over Easter. The season was balancing on a knife-edge. With seconds to go at Wembley, Oldham led in the FA Cup semi-final and United's dreams were threatening to disintegrate.

Aston Villa had already ended hopes of a domestic Treble with victory in the League Cup final and the Reds were not prepared to admit defeat in the most famous cup competition of all. Hughes delivered a show-stopping volley in the 119th minute and the mood was transformed. Some argue Oldham never recovered from the late setback. The replay was a formality and a 4-1 battering of the Latics saw Giggs notch the final strike to add to a previous effort in the League Cup semi-final against Sheffield Wednesday.

In the title run-in, his pace embarrassed Gary Kelly to cement another impressive win at Leeds' Elland Road, which was understandably beginning to hold fewer fears, and a vital winner at Ipswich Town, converting an Irwin cross, ensured he would provide the telling contribution en route to the retention of the title by a final margin of eight points.

Chelsea may have done the league double over the Reds, with Gavin Peacock scoring the only goal on both occasions, but they were no match for Ferguson's men in a rain-soaked FA Cup final. A 4-0 hammering meant a first-ever Double for United, and Giggs was a star in one of the club's greatest-ever sides, finishing second top-scorer in the league behind Cantona and recording a 17-goal haul in all competitions that he never bettered.

The XI that took the field at Wembley is the one commonly identified with this glorious campaign: Schmeichel; Parker, Bruce,

In January 1994, victory over Everton – secured by Ryan's header – marked the death of Sir Matt Busby, whose football mantra lived on through Alex Ferguson.

Ryan and Paul Ince show their premeditated celebrations after the Welshman's vital late-season clincher at Elland Road.

Pallister, Irwin; Kanchelskis, Keane, Ince, Giggs; Hughes, Cantona. Sharpe was a late substitute but was, by now, playing second fiddle to Giggs and the jet-heeled Kanchelskis. In paying Sharpe a compliment on his return from injury that season, Ferguson revealed the esteem he had for the younger of the left-wingers: 'The boy Sharpe is improving all the time. He's not a Ryan Giggs, but he's becoming a top player through his improved passing.'

Giggs suffered a series of colds towards the end of the term, resulting in him having his tonsils removed, and perhaps it hinted the physical endeavours were taking their toll. With United firmly established as England's top dogs and pursuing a third successive title, commercial distractions (including hosting his own TV show, *Ryan Giggs' Soccer Skills*) and the start of an ongoing battle with niggling injuries curtailed his progress. Some were too quick to question his longevity, reverting to the earlier scepticism regarding his limitless promise. As a high-profile sportsman, there was pressure to maintain the high standards that had been set and further them.

Both Giggs and Sharpe were pin-ups, with their appeal stretching beyond the confines of the game. They would joke about the attention from young female followers, with Sharpe calculating around 75 per cent of his fan mail was from 13- and 14-year-old girls. 'They write things like "I love you", and "You're dead fit",' he laughed. The amount of cards and presents from supporters overwhelmed Giggs when he turned twenty-one later in 1994, and his grandfather was charged with the task of dealing with the avalanche of mail and gifts.

At least it provided more ammunition for mirth among his elder colleagues, including Gary Pallister, who scoffed at the suggestion that the Welshman was fashionable, cool and something of a heart-throb. 'I know all the bad habits he's got,' said the centre-back. 'Sorry, I can't tell you what they are. I've also seen Ryan do a decent Cossack dance on a table, but I don't know whether that's considered trendy right now!'

Eric Cantona earns the acclaim of his colleagues as Chelsea are brushed aside by the champions in the 1994 FA Cup final to seal the club's first Double.

Back-to-back champions and now cup winners to boot, Ryan and the Reds take to the streets of Manchester on an open-top bus parade.

# Ryan Giggs
## The Man for All Seasons

As an advertiser's dream, once the shackles were loosened, Giggs was persuaded to give his name to various products and ventures, and he admits it did have an impact in draining some of his natural energy. Although wisely acknowledging a need to cut back, particularly on the more physically demanding projects, the media glare was threatening to overshadow his performances on the field.

Fate would play a part and provide some good fortune in this respect. David Beckham embraced the celebrity lifestyle after his emergence and it deflected much of the attention. 'I was trying to keep out of the limelight and then, obviously, Becks came into the team and everything happened with that,' acknowledged Giggs. 'I suppose it was good timing for me.'

Nevertheless, the press required a leading man as football enjoyed a great renaissance in the public consciousness, leaving behind the dark days of hooliganism, with all-seater stadiums ensuring a friendlier, more family-oriented atmosphere. The boom started post-Italia 90, with Paul Gascoigne heralded as a new national idol, his tears in the semi-final against West Germany projecting his personality to a wider audience beyond devoted football fans. Yet his tragic implosion in the FA Cup final less than a year later, with a serious injury ensuring he would arguably never recapture his previous brilliance, meant there was a void to be filled before Beckham and, later, Wayne Rooney would face similar adulation, attention and scrutiny. Giggs was destined to be that man, and had to contend with these external influences for a difficult spell.

'I didn't embrace that lifestyle, like Becks,' he explained. 'I was comfortable with the football and the photo shoots, but I was never comfortable with people following me around. I felt that kind of attention would have negatively affected my football. I made a conscious decision that I didn't really like it and just wanted to keep a low profile.'

Of course, there were probably no lingering doubts behind the scenes, but his measured finish against Wimbledon in August, in the

86th minute of a simple 3-0 win, proved to be his only league goal
of the 1994-95 season from 29 starts – a remarkable statistic considering
his output a year earlier. There were two straightforward strikes against
IFK Gothenburg in the Champions League too, but the European
adventure was to be short-lived again. He featured in only one of the
last four matches of the group stages, and that was a 4-0 schooling
by Barcelona as the foreigners rule severely handicapped Ferguson's
team selections.

At Ipswich in September, the injury problems started to flare.
Calf, ankle, Achilles and, particularly, hamstring worries stymied the
winger's contribution. Ryan played in only one of the next four league
games after the Portman Road reverse and, after being involved as
Kanchelskis stole the show with a hat-trick in a 5-0 Manchester derby-
day massacre, he did not reappear until another defeat, at home to
Nottingham Forest, a little over a week before Christmas.

United were not in top gear but reduced the gap on leaders
Blackburn to two points with a 1-0 win over Rovers on 22 January,
a game that marked Andy Cole's debut following his shock record
move from Newcastle United. The crucial goal came in the 80th minute
after Giggs's run was initially halted by Henning Berg. He recovered to
make a trademark sliding tackle on the Norwegian and delivered an
inviting cross for Cantona to spear his header past Tim Flowers.

The Reds were primed to overtake Kenny Dalglish's expensively
assembled side, but disaster struck in controversial fashion just three
days later at Crystal Palace when Cantona reacted to a goading fan
after being sent off. The Frenchman's kung-fu kick rocked the sporting
world and he was, ultimately, banned for nine months after being
spared a custodial sentence in court. The simple theory is this was the
reason for a first campaign without silverware since 1989, but, as is
often the case, the truth was surely more complex.

United still won the next three league games and, after losing
at Everton, hit a record nine goals past Ipswich without reply, Cole

claiming five of them. Giggs enjoyed himself that day, and was regaining his previous sparkle. 'Young players like Ryan can lose confidence a bit sometimes and maybe that's what happened to him before Christmas,' conceded Irwin. 'But, when he's on form, there's nobody better than him in the game.'

Giggs continued in the team until making a final league appearance in a goalless draw with Leeds on 2 April as he suffered another hamstring injury. Missing the run-in would be agonising, as he could only watch from the sidelines as the drama unfolded. On a frantic final day, Blackburn losing at Liverpool meant victory at West Ham would snatch top spot for the Reds. United laid siege to Ludek Miklosko's goal, but the Czech keeper twice denied Cole in the closing stages and a 1-1 draw relinquished the Reds' grip on the Premier League trophy.

It was the absence of Giggs and not Cantona that was on Ferguson's mind. 'It's arguable he could have won us the league at the death,' the Scot mused as he had to lift his dejected troops for the FA Cup final with Everton six days later. Another inspired goalkeeping display, this time by Giggs's Wales colleague Neville Southall, made for another miserable afternoon. Ryan clearly was nowhere near fully fit, but he had started every match of the cup run, scoring against Wrexham, and, when he replaced Steve Bruce at half time, it ensured his last three outings of 1994-95 were all in the competition. It was a low point for somebody so accustomed to winning as he trudged off the pitch in some pain after Paul Rideout's goal settled a low-key final.

The manager's response to the double disappointment was to rip up his much-exalted team. Kanchelskis, Ince and Hughes all departed, making space for an influx of Giggs's pals from the FA Youth Cup-winning side – Beckham, Nicky Butt and Paul Scholes. Gary Neville would oust Paul Parker from the right-back slot and his younger brother Phil also made the breakthrough. The sweeping changes rocked the supporters and the press alike, while Giggs felt a sense of loss at seeing Ince head to Italy to join Inter Milan.

Ince had even allowed his friend to move into his family home, sharing a room with toddler Tom, whom he would later play against. 'Giggsy was my best mate,' Ince told the *Daily Telegraph*. 'He came from a split home, so maybe that's one reason we understood each other. He ended up coming to stay with me for six months in Bramhall. That's where we built up our friendship. We used to practise those goal celebrations in the bedroom.'

Giggs was not part of the new-look side that opened the campaign with a 3-1 defeat at Aston Villa, prompting pundit Alan Hansen to famously declare you win nothing with kids. Ferguson wanted to ease the injured Welshman back into the fold, and he made a couple of rare Reserves outings against Notts County and Liverpool, scoring in both fixtures. He was introduced for the last quarter of an hour of a sweet victory at champions Blackburn, following Beckham's winner, and also came off the bench to good effect at Everton, netting the decider seven minutes after replacing Scholes. It was a special moment and one that resonated with Ferguson for some time as he saw the players engulf their popular teammate and share his elation at notching his first league goal for over a year.

'I knew that the majority of that youth side would play in the first team, but not five or six at the same time,' admitted Ryan, who was enjoying the reunion with his friends. He did not have to wait long for his next goal as, in the next league outing, he slid home a cross from the latest debutant, Terry Cooke, during a 3-0 win against Bolton Wanderers.

Suddenly, the 21-year-old was a senior figure to some of his colleagues (he had already notched up almost 200 appearances for the club by the start of the season) and his strong personality was coming to the fore. Parker remembers learning never to push his teammate too far when it came to any dressing-room banter. 'He would always just smile but, if there was an issue, you knew he was getting angry,' explained the defender. 'His eyes would go.

We would call him "Norman Bates" [the character from *Psycho*] because of his mad eyes. There was this tough side to him and a line you couldn't cross. But nobody could say a bad word about him, because you'd know to leave it there. It was a bit like Eric – you knew where you stood in certain situations when he'd signal enough was enough.'

Cantona's fuse, of course, was far shorter than Ryan's but he served his time, enjoying aspects of his community service, and returned from the ban in a blaze of publicity against Liverpool, setting up a goal for Nicky Butt after two minutes. United had already been dumped out of Europe by Rotor Volgograd, despite a late Peter Schmeichel equaliser at Old Trafford, and on course to be humbled by York City in the League Cup, with Giggs on the field for every minute of both legs.

A brace by Robbie Fowler threatened to ruin a rousing occasion at Old Trafford, only for Giggs to outsprint Jamie Redknapp and draw a clumsy challenge from the England international inside the area. It was an opportunity Cantona was never going to pass up and his penalty was not to be the last time he would beat David James in the 1995-96 campaign. Maybe the return of Cantona stole the limelight to such an extent that Giggs could concentrate on recapturing his own best form.

'At the beginning of the season I was trying to avoid getting injured,' he conceded. 'In particular, the niggling injuries that gave me such a disappointing season last year. I was only playing two weeks at a time back then.'

A solo effort at Chelsea, when he tied Steve Clarke in knots, harked back to his teenage years and he netted twice in the first four minutes at home to Southampton, the opener quickly taking its place as the fastest United goal on record. However, five matches without a win allowed Kevin Keegan's Newcastle to pull clear in the title race and painful defeats at Liverpool and Leeds, with Giggs absent for the latter, led to the feeling at Christmas that the marauding Magpies were primed to land their first championship since 1927.

Eric Harrison and United's emerging youth prospects, the Class of '92 (left to right: Ryan, Nicky Butt, David Beckham, Gary Neville, Phil Neville, Paul Scholes and Terry Cooke).

Andy Cole hails Ryan's contribution to a vital Eric Cantona goal at West Ham United as the Reds begin to reel in league leaders Newcastle.

United reduced the gap to seven points with a vital 2-0 victory over the Tynesiders on 27 December but, after Ryan side-footed in an Irwin assist for the eventual winner against QPR, a 4-1 hiding at Tottenham on New Year's Day, with Kevin Pilkington replacing Schmeichel at half time, got 1996 off to a woeful start.

Another unappealing visit to the Boleyn Ground in East London on a freezing Monday evening looked capable of derailing United for good. The Reds trailed Newcastle by 12 points and had not won at the Hammers' home since the previous decade. However, the priceless 1-0 triumph featured a moment of magic from Giggs that lives long in the memory. Julian Dicks perhaps deserved his reputation for kicking wingers first and asking questions later, but was left flummoxed by a single touch of the ball that spun it into the winger's path as he turned sharply to accelerate and circumnavigate the left-back. Once Cole returned a pass into the Welshman's path, Dicks was out of the equation, and Giggs spotted Cantona with his arm aloft beyond the far post. A low cross evaded Sharpe at full stretch but, from a difficult angle, United's No. 7 illustrated his composure and there was no chance of Miklosko thwarting the Reds again.

It was a wonderful goal, one typical of Ferguson's United, and it sealed the first of five consecutive league wins, with one against Everton including another strike by Giggs, to apply pressure on Newcastle ahead of the visit to St James' Park in early March. Cantona, inevitably, ended the Magpies' 100 per cent record on their home patch, but much of the credit went to Schmeichel for a heroic performance between the posts. Remarkably, the lead was down to a single point, even if Keegan's men did have a game in hand, and Cantona simply inspired the youthful team with a string of vital goalscoring interventions.

The Frenchman's penalty at Manchester City, however, was not as important as the 78th-minute winner rocketed in by Giggs. Blues defender Keith Curle vocally urged his opponent to shoot from distance, then watched on as the ball hurtled into Eike Immel's top corner.

After a moment's hesitation, wondering why the ground had gone so quiet, Ryan feels able to celebrate his stunning derby winner at Maine Road.

Maine Road was stunned into silence, to the point that the goalscorer feared his effort had been disallowed. His next goal was, in comparison, rather unimportant as it was a consolation in a game at Southampton best remembered for United changing their grey shirts at half time.

Defeat at The Dell would not deny the Reds, as Leeds were overcome 1-0 on a tense night at Old Trafford, despite being forced to field Lucas Radebe in goal for 73 minutes after Mark Beeney was sent off, with the South African centre-back making good saves from Giggs and others in a red shirt. Ferguson was upset with the effort the ten men had shown, on the back of six defeats in seven games, and wondered if they would show similar resolve in their next outing against Newcastle. It led to Keegan's televised rant on Sky Sports after his own side did beat the Yorkshiremen, but the title rivals' contrasting results against Nottingham Forest would prove key, with Giggs scoring in a 5-0 United win before Newcastle were held to a 1-1 draw at the City Ground. The trophy was coming home if defeat could be avoided at Middlesbrough on the final day. A 3-0 triumph won the league 'down by the Riverside', as the fans chanted, with Ryan's late thunderbolt with his trusty left foot even earning the sporting applause of the home supporters.

This time United approached the FA Cup final, reached for the third successive year, in a relaxed mood and determined to upset a Liverpool side that had finished third and collected four points from Ferguson's men. A stale tactical battle ensued with few chances until James punched out a Beckham corner and skipper Cantona volleyed through a forest of bodies for the dramatic winner.

Ferguson had experimented at times by asking Giggs to play a more central role during the course of the season, partly to accommodate Scholes, and often supported by the more defensive-minded Keane and Butt. It was another step in his evolution as a modern footballer and his flexibility would present more options to his manager in terms of his formation, plus enable him to gradually adapt his game as his lightning pace decreased over time. This tight

Pals Nicky Butt and Paul Scholes join Ryan in parading the FA Cup in 1996, as the Reds celebrate a second Double in three seasons.

affair at Wembley was another illustration of his ability to carry out instructions and influence the biggest of matches.

'We said to Ryan that maybe in this game he should try and vary going inside the park and out, because there were problems going infield,' revealed Ferguson afterwards. 'That advice proved correct because he made a lot of good runs in behind the midfield and behind Jason McAteer and Mark Wright. It is easy to forget he was a member of the 1992 FA Youth Cup-winning side when his consistency and quality of play shows so much maturity.'

The 1996 Double triumph owed much to Cantona, the returning idol, and it is only right that his redemption was the main narrative at its climax. However, in the background, Giggs had re-emerged as one of the team's leading lights. In a vote held in the club's official magazine in the summer, he was the second-most popular player in the view of the fans.

Hence, there was clearly never any suggestion he would be part of the traditional close-season squad alterations, but more senior figures departed, including experienced defenders Bruce and Parker. 'One of the greatest things about signing for United from QPR was I never had to play against Ryan in any season,' smiled right-back Parker. More pertinently, left-winger Sharpe was also deemed surplus to requirements and left for Leeds. 'I never held it against him,' said the departing winger. 'It didn't ever become personal. There was never any animosity between us. We were different players. I was just unfortunate he was in my position.'

Incredibly, Sharpe's exit meant only Brian McClair, Pallister, Irwin and Schmeichel had been in the team longer, emphasising the rapid nature of United's evolution. In his half-decade in senior football, Giggs had sampled plentiful highs and lows, and there would be plenty more of both to come.

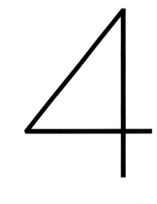

# Toast of the Continent

With three Premier League titles, two FA Cups and a League Cup to show for five seasons' work, English football held few new challenges for United and Giggs. The continent, however, remained an itch to be scratched. Alex Ferguson's Double winners were primed for a third tilt at the new-look UEFA Champions League, having failed to get past the group stage on their previous two attempts.

In order to attain sufficient squad depth for continued domestic dominance and making the step up in Europe, United's ranks were swollen by five new summer recruits: Jordi Cruyff being the most renowned and Karel Poborsky perhaps the most exciting, following his Euro 96 heroics with beaten finalists Czech Republic. Norwegians Ronny Johnsen and Ole Gunnar Solskjaer, plus Dutch goalkeeper Raimond van der Gouw, were almost total unknowns. UEFA had changed the rules on foreign players, meaning there was

no longer any bar on the number who could be fielded by a side in their competitions.

For Solskjaer, the role of newcomer forced him to take a sustained look at the dressing room dynamic as he found his place within his new surroundings. Giggs, still only twenty-two but a first-team fixture for half a decade, aligned himself with peers who had followed his path through the youth ranks. 'The class of '92 lads – Giggsy, Becks, Gary, Phil, Butty, Scholesy – were together all the time,' says the Norwegian. 'They were a real core within that dressing room. What was good to see in training, though, was that it wasn't like: "I'm not touching him, we're best mates"; it was really competitive and good for the whole group that we had them who had gone through the whole system. They were some of the best human beings I've come across and what those lads brought to the dressing room was really, really healthy to have.'

Less healthy was Giggs's physical state as 1996-97 began, with lingering concerns surrounding his hamstring. So, as a precautionary measure, he sat out the Premier League opener at Wimbledon, in which David Beckham scored from inside his own half. Though his return began with a pair of 2-2 home draws against Everton and Blackburn Rovers as United searched for form, defeats were few and far between. Personally, he sampled only one Premier League loss all term, and six in all competitions. The first two were inflicted by Juventus in the Champions League group stage, with a particularly harrowing reverse suffered in Turin. United lost only 1-0, but were comprehensively schooled by their hosts, with Giggs in particular learning valuable lessons both on and off the pitch.

'I had a shocker,' he admitted. 'I kept dribbling with the ball, Didier Deschamps would take it off me, pass it to Zinedine Zidane who'd give it to Del Piero, and they'd be in on our goal every time. The gaffer had a right go at me at half time, and I had a dig back. I didn't feel it was all my fault. We argued about it, and he took me off. So I guess that was an argument I lost!'

Ryan is in the thick of things against Everton, on this occasion finding himself thwarted by former Wales teammate Neville Southall.

An assured finish against Rapid Vienna helps clinch qualification from the Champions League group stages.

The residual irritation of a frustrating evening in Turin was soon vented. Three days later, Giggs notched his first goal of the season in a routine 4-1 home win over Nottingham Forest, only for his persistent hamstring issues to resurface midway through October, while United were still unbeaten domestically. In his month-long absence, Giggs had to watch on in horror as the Reds' confidence was shattered by four damaging defeats against Newcastle, Southampton, Fenerbahce and Chelsea. Though his return coincided with a much-needed league victory over Arsenal, another reverse against Juventus left United needing three points at Rapid Vienna in their group finale to have any chance of reaching the knockout stages of the Champions League, with a Fenerbahce slip in Turin also key to the deal.

Juventus maintained their end of the bargain with a routine win in the Stadio Delle Alpi, and Giggs proved key as United finally progressed to the knockout stages. Peter Schmeichel's wonder save from Rene Wagner prevented an early deficit, but it was Giggs who made the vital breakthrough before half time, latching on to a sublime through-ball from Eric Cantona and steering home an unerring finish. Cantona added a second after the break to wrap up progress and a daunting tie with dark horses Porto, who had beaten established powerhouses AC Milan home and away in their own group campaign.

In the interim, United's assault on the domestic game continued apace. Between November's defeat to Chelsea and the March arrival of Porto at Old Trafford, the Reds went 16 league games unbeaten and established a four-point lead over Liverpool, as Giggs scored in January wins over Coventry and Wimbledon, with a superb right-footed curler and a deftly looped header respectively. The only blotch on his record was a shock FA Cup exit against the Dons, but that was forgotten a month later when Portugal's finest pitched up in Manchester.

While Ryan was unhappy with his own form throughout 1996-97 as a whole – terming it 'too stop-start' – he put in a performance against Porto which would stand comparison with any display throughout his twenty-four years in the United team. Deployed in central midfield alongside Johnsen and instructed to break from deep and utilise spaces created by the runs of Andy Cole and Solskjaer – himself re-stationed to Giggs's left-wing berth – the Welshman was a phenomenon all night, bagging the third goal as United built an insurmountable 4-0 first-leg lead.

'Giggs produced one of the best performances by a United player in Europe since George Best destroyed Benfica in the Stadium of Light in 1966.'

**David Lacey**
*Guardian*

'It's probably the best game I've ever had for United,' he later said. 'My passing was spot on, I was winning tackles and the satisfaction and exhilaration that comes from playing like that is huge. The gaffer said afterwards he'd never seen me play better. It was one of those occasions when we attacked from every angle, interchanging positions, and our play came from every direction. Everything we tried came off and we were all over them. They never stood a chance.'

It was Giggs's first performance on the European stage to provoke unanimous acclaim. The *Guardian*'s David Lacey gushed: 'Giggs produced one of the best performances by a United player in Europe since George Best destroyed Benfica in the Stadium of Light in 1966.' He went on to highlight 'the consistency with which he instigated attacks, beat opponents with the ball and created space with

shrewdly angled runs'. Alex Ferguson, meanwhile, could only marvel: 'Sensational! What a performance from the boy!'

The display came at a cost, however. 'In big, high-tempo European games when I played well, I knew I'd suffer for it afterwards,' admitted Giggs. 'That was the worst it has ever felt.' He was sidelined for the subsequent game – a shock 2-1 Premier League defeat at Sunderland – and the second leg in Porto, and his involvement in the season's climax would be further decimated by injury. After United confirmed a Champions League semi-final tie against Borussia Dortmund, he would start only three more games: a key win at Everton, his first league defeat of the season at home to Derby and the first leg of the double-header against Dortmund.

Ahead of the meeting in Germany, Giggs was afflicted by an unknown problem in his stomach, which compromised his power and explosiveness. He started at the Westfalenstadion, but was a shadow of his usual self. It would transpire that he required a double hernia operation, but the decision was taken to delay the procedure in case he was needed in the final games of the campaign. He was – in the second leg of the Dortmund tie – as United sought to overturn a 1-0 deficit. However, despite producing enough chances to win several games, the Reds slipped to a second defeat and exited 2-0 on aggregate.

Giggs, clearly unfit throughout his substitute cameo, later admitted that he should have played no part and he remained on the sidelines as Ferguson's men closed out their title defence to notch a fourth domestic rule in five years. 'How we didn't beat Dortmund, with all the chances we had, is still a mystery,' said Gary Pallister. 'Giggsy clearly wasn't fully fit and if he had been, that might have made a difference, but there was no point dwelling on it. We could only blame ourselves.'

Despite the glory of preserving the league table's status quo, the season did not constitute a success for a club always eyeing the next step.

Ryan turns in one of his greatest individual displays from a central midfield position as United thrash FC Porto at Old Trafford.

Celebrating another league title with Eric Cantona, Nicky Butt, David Beckham, Phil Neville, Gary Neville, Paul Scholes and Roy Keane.

Failure to see through a European campaign of such promise prompted a mood of chagrin, which was only heightened when team talisman Cantona announced his shock retirement. 'Life with Eric was one long surprise,' shrugged Giggs. 'You never knew what he would do next.'

The Frenchman, for his part, had relished his half-decade playing alongside his Welsh colleague. 'Sometimes players like to run, so they run. They are quick, but to be there at the right moment is different. You have to have a lot of anticipation. I liked to give the ball like a present to somebody; I didn't like it when I gave a good pass to somebody who never scores goals. To play with Ryan Giggs was different, because I knew when I received the ball that he would find the space and run faster than anybody, then afterwards he would have the skill to score the goal.'

Despite that glaring validation from one of modern football's true greats, Giggs was aware that his haul of just five goals in 37 appearances, punctuated by undulating form, was not sufficient. His aim for the future was simple: a return to personal splendour. For long periods of 1997-98, that looked inevitable as he rediscovered his scintillating best form, prompting Sir Bobby Charlton to proffer his own reasons behind the youngster's travails over the previous three years.

In a candid interview with the *Daily Mirror*, he said: 'It was all down to Ryan's personal integrity. He was trying too hard to do well for Manchester United. He had suddenly become an extremely wealthy young man and big-money contracts were flying at him from all angles. He was a high-profile personality all over the world. But he wanted to give his money's worth. And he made it difficult, almost impossible, for himself. He set himself fantastic standards. He wanted to run too fast, score spectacular goals every match, beat too many players and turn it on all the time.

'He wanted to do too many difficult things when it just wasn't necessary. It was nothing to do with being bigheaded. He's just not like that – it was what he felt the club expected of him. And he came off the rails. But we are quite sensible at Old Trafford and Alex Ferguson recognised what was happening. He had the patience. He knew that Ryan was a sprinter, that he was like a greyhound that you can't keep on flogging into action. He understood it wouldn't be long before Ryan got going again. And once Ryan had realised we didn't expect him to perform like he felt he should to prove his worth, it was all OK. Look at him now. He's thinking about the game a little bit more. He was a victim of his own honesty and willingness to give it his all to show that he wasn't over-rated.

'When you have a rare super talent like Ryan, Alex is not likely to let it go awry for too long. He's only a youngster – but the older he gets, the more appreciation he has of his own ability. And he will only get better. We want him at United for a long time to come – not only for the sake of the club, but for the fans who have a right to be able to marvel at such a sensational talent.'

And marvel they did, as Giggs turned in a series of fine early-season displays either in his customary left-wing role or in the central berth that worked so spectacularly against Porto. Chasing a third straight title, United also began the campaign in fine fettle, heading the Premier League table and conceding just four times in the opening ten games across all competitions. A first defeat of the term came in late September at Leeds United – with Giggs rested to preserve him for the visit of Juventus four days later – but the reverse at Elland Road carried the greater cost of losing Roy Keane to cruciate knee ligament damage.

The Irishman's absence rocked the Reds ahead of the visit of Marcello Lippi's side, yet the squad retained a steely determination that Serie A's finest could and would be vanquished, Keane or no Keane. As if to underline Juventus's status as European football's benchmark, Del Piero put the visitors ahead after just 19 seconds to stun Old Trafford. Giggs, deployed centrally behind Teddy Sheringham (who had joined the club the previous summer, as a replacement for

# Ryan Giggs
## The Man for All Seasons

The cup competitions would continue to house the winger's outstanding contributions. A non-stop performance yielded dividends as United gradually wore down Liverpool to progress with two late, late FA Cup fourth-round goals, but just as the Reds were well set to compete on all fronts, a nightmarish dose of déjà vu threatened to rob Ferguson of Giggs for the second year in succession. Once again, the Welshman sustained a hamstring injury during a February win over Derby at Old Trafford but, this time, United's fears were allayed. Giggs would miss only two games and the Reds coped comfortably in his absence, beating Nottingham Forest 8-1 and advancing to the quarter-finals of the FA Cup at the expense of Fulham.

The winger's return to the starting line-up brought immediate dividends with a priceless late winner at Coventry City; a smash-and-grab performance achieved in the fine margins which would make or break United's season. Yet two games after returning to the starting XI at Highfield Road, Giggs sustained a broken nose via the elbow of Inter Milan defender Javier Zanetti, and while he was able to play on through a hugely impressive 2-0 victory over the bookies' favourites for the Champions League, the winger sat out the next game, a drab FA Cup draw with Chelsea. He returned for the victorious replay at Stamford Bridge but continued to yo-yo between the pitch and the treatment table as the season entered its nitty-gritty phase. The presence of Blomqvist allowed United to plough on in his absence, with points taken from Everton and Wimbledon, and Giggs's next outing, after a triumphant second leg draw in the San Siro, was the semi-final first-leg tie with old foes Juventus.

While optimism was high ahead of the clash at Old Trafford, the Italians' pedigree – a fourth straight Champions League final was in their reach – was without question, and Marcello Lippi's side deservedly led 1-0 at half time through Antonio Conte. The visitors were edging the midfield battle, where their trio of Deschamps, Zidane and Edgar Davids outnumbered Keane and Scholes. Ferguson left Giggs and Beckham in

no doubt that they had to contribute more defensively after the break if United were to turn the tide. Sure enough, after United had mustered a final half-hour of growing pressure, Beckham's hooked cross eventually landed at the feet of Giggs and the Welshman was able to thud a crisp, close-range finish into the roof of the Stretford End net. 'Ryan's goal has given us a chance over in Turin,' admitted a relieved Ferguson. Not that the manager's thoughts could wander that far forward, with an FA Cup semi-final clash with reigning champions Arsenal to come just four days after Juve's visit to Old Trafford.

Giggs would ultimately play the decisive role in one of English football's all-time classic cup ties, yet the greatest goal of his career only came to pass after he himself was punished by an inexplicable decision from officials when the sides first locked horns at Villa Park. A goalless draw was notable for an extraordinary decision by referee David Elleray – on the say-so of his linesman, Graham Atkins – to disallow Keane's first-half goal for offside. Yorke was penalised for being ahead of play when, 15 yards away, Giggs touched the ball past Lee Dixon in order to resume possession and cross into the area. He duly did, Yorke headed on and Keane slammed home a finish, only to see the goal chalked off on Atkins' recommendation.

'It was absolutely ridiculous,' scoffed Ferguson. 'I have watched it on TV and it's quite amazing. But it doesn't matter. It wasn't a goal and we have just got to get on with it.' The United manager was loathe to crowbar another high-stakes match into an already brimming fixture list, but nevertheless used the short turnaround time – just three days – between the original tie and the replay to engage Giggs in an incredibly timely chat. 'He called me into his office to remind me that it was my pace and direct running at defenders that made me the player I was,' revealed Ryan. 'He did it maybe once a season, just making a point to remind me of my strengths.'

Whether Ferguson's pep talk was given with the Villa Park replay in mind, only he knows. Certainly, Giggs was benched for the first hour, rested with one eye on the trip to Turin looming just a week later, and he only entered a barnstorming match when Blomqvist began to tire under growing Arsenal pressure. Seven minutes after the substitute's introduction, Dennis Bergkamp struck a deflected equaliser to cancel out Beckham's stunning opener – the first goal Arsenal's defence had conceded in 11½ hours of football. Before long, Nicolas Anelka had a goal disallowed for offside, Keane was dismissed for a second booking and Schmeichel saved a last-gasp Bergkamp penalty to take the tie to extra time. Amid it all, Giggs had been a peripheral figure, rarely coming into contact with the ball and invariably doing little with it when he did.

Perhaps that low-key contribution explains Patrick Vieira's weary pass straight into the inviting space in front of Giggs, ten yards inside the United half, four minutes into the second period of extra time. 'From nowhere, as if he's just popped up out of the ground, Ryan got on the ball,' recalled Ferguson. 'Steve McClaren, myself and Jim Ryan are going: "Take it to the corner flag, go on, run it to the corner flag."' Behind Giggs, similar cries were coming from his supporting full-back. 'I was so tired, I just couldn't get on the overlap,' admits Phil Neville, 'so I was saying: "Go on, just run!" He ran, and I shouted: "Keep going, keep going!" And it was like slow motion.'

Though fronted by an entire half littered with Arsenal shirts, Giggs continued to motor forward. Six touches had taken him 30 yards before a dip of the shoulder accounted for Vieira, and suddenly he was fronted with three-quarters of Arsenal's infamously stoic defence: Dixon, Martin Keown and Tony Adams. The latter hung back to assess the situation, aware that Scholes was sprinting into the area behind him, bellowing for a cross. That left Dixon and Keown, backpedalling and awkwardly aligned, but still imposing enough to seemingly have control of the situation. Until another shoulder drop flipped their positions, putting the right-back infield of his centre-back. Having craftily manipulated a position of power, Giggs made his move: a quick switch from his left foot on to his right and a burst at full throttle took him into space inside

the area. Adams, also foxed by the quick shimmy, made his move too late and was superfluous to the situation as Giggs, for the first time in 40 yards, had time to look up and assess the situation. Though England's goalkeeper blocked the goal and the angle was unforgiving, he made a simple decision: hit it! Hard. Seaman's feet had barely left the ground as the ball ripped into the net high above his head. Cue disbelief in every single soul involved, then utter pandemonium.

Giggs, still full sprint, was suddenly semi-naked and whirling his shirt around his head, as United fans spilled on to the field and teammates hurtled towards him. Seaman, Keown and Adams watched from prostrate positions as United supporters and players mingled frenziedly. On the touchline, Ferguson and McClaren beamed as they hastily concocted a plan for the remaining 10 minutes of time, which were seen out in a euphoric haze as the Reds booked a Wembley date with Newcastle United. Giggs's evening was stripped of some gloss as he suffered a painful foot injury after a Dixon challenge, but he was spared the need to transport himself anywhere as United fans swarmed about him and chaired their match-winner from the field. Despite leaving the ground on crutches, Giggs was walking on air and didn't grasp the enormity of his strike until later, long after the match.

'It was a blur; it all happened so quickly,' he says. 'As I left the ground, I remember a few reporters coming over to me and asking if it was the best goal I'd ever scored. I told them I didn't know, because the thought hadn't occurred to me. I got home that night, watched it back and hadn't realised that I'd picked the ball up that far out. It was all a blur, all instinct at the time. It makes it better that it was a proper football match against a proper team. There was so much history between the two teams, the stakes were so high, and they were such good opponents, too. Seaman was like Schmeichel in the way he made the goal look so small, so when I got through, that really was the only place I could have put the finish.'

Giggs's greatest-ever goal is saved for a special occasion as he settles the last FA Cup semi-final replay with a sensational strike against Arsenal.

Newcastle's Rob Lee trips Ryan at Wembley, but the Reds still stroll to victory in the 1999 FA Cup final. Two down, one to go.

With an FA Cup final berth secured, a slender advantage at the head of the Premier League table and a Champions League semi-final decider to come, suddenly talk of the Treble was rife. The mood in the United camp was one of giddy anticipation before each fixture, and Giggs's teammates took great delight in regularly reminding him of his hirsute celebration at Villa Park. 'He was called Captain Caveman for quite a while after that,' revealed Denis Irwin.

While more than happy to absorb the dressing room's mirth in return for his moment of genius, Giggs cut a frustrated figure as his injured foot healed, and he missed the next six games. Juventus were heroically beaten on their own turf, while the title race played out in such a fashion that when he returned for the penultimate match of the league season, at Blackburn, a victory would put the Reds three points clear with a game to go. In typical United fashion, a goalless draw took matters down to the wire, while also relegating former assistant manager Kidd. Mixed emotions infiltrated Ewood Park's away dressing room as Giggs and several other players considered the impact of the result on their former coach, but United's need for points took precedence. Now the Reds had a slender advantage going into the final day of the Premier League season.

So, with three games of an absorbing season remaining, United could conceivably win nothing, everything or achieve a level of glory in between. Back to full fitness, Giggs featured in all three games. First up was a nervy comeback win over Tottenham to regain the Premier League, followed by a routine stroll against Newcastle to take the FA Cup and notch a third domestic Double in six years. Giggs featured on the left wing in both games, but knew he would be relocated for the biggest encounter of all: the Champions League final against Bayern Munich. The cost of United's progress in Turin was the loss of Keane and Scholes to suspension, enforcing a substantial rejig across the midfield four. Butt was a shoo-in to start in one of two central berths, while Giggs was strongly considered to partner his close friend, before

The big one. Ryan finally gets his hands on the European Cup on the grandest night of his career – the unforgettable, Treble-clinching victory over Bayern Munich in Barcelona.

goalkeeper Iker Casillas, then just eighteen, and Vicente Del Bosque's side were home and hosed soon after half time through Raul's quickfire brace, despite a late United rally to bring the scoreline back to 2-3. 'The gaffer had said that 0-0 over there wasn't any kind of scoreline, and he was absolutely right,' admitted Giggs. 'Their players weren't the sort to come to Old Trafford and be intimidated.'

Solace was provided three days later when victory at Southampton retained the Premier League title with four games to spare, rendering the remainder of the season nothing more than a chase to notch 100 league goals. Giggs scored in the 3-2 victory at Watford, but United would ultimately fall three goals short of the century, winning the title by 18 points from an Arsenal side beaten by just a solitary point a year earlier.

With seven goals from 44 appearances, two major honours and a sustained spell of his best form, the winger could reflect on a triumphant personal campaign, even if there was a general sense of anti-climax around the club after failing to emulate the Treble. The Reds would be chasing a repeat of that high in vain for years, occasionally coming close but never quite matching the clean sweep of May 1999.

The template set in 1999-2000 would be closely followed in 2000-01, both by Giggs and United. Once more, the Reds' No. 11 continued to bewitch opponents at will, with his best displays reserved for the Champions League, while their rule over England's top division could not be transferred to the continental game to the same extent.

It was on a rare instance of dropped points that Ryan's outstanding moment of the campaign arose. Moments after equalising for the Reds at Charlton, the 27-year-old provoked gasps of amazement around The Valley as he looped an incredible 50-yard shot against the underside of Dean Kiely's crossbar. Though the ever-alert Ole Gunnar Solskjaer took the spoils by tucking away the rebound, the post-match plaudits were reserved for the goal's provider. 'You have to admire the audacity Ryan showed,' grinned

Giggs turns in a man-of-the-match performance as United overcome Palmeiras in the Intercontinental Cup to become England's first world champions.

United's controversial Club World Championship campaign took Ryan to the world famous Maracana Stadium, but England's finest were unable to triumph in Brazil.

# Ryan Giggs
## The Man for All Seasons

Ferguson, despite seeing his side squander a two-goal lead in a 3-3 draw. 'Not many players would have sensed that opportunity to try and score from that distance, let alone come within an inch or two of doing it.'

That snapshot of genius validated Giggs's inclusion on the 50-man shortlist for the Ballon d'Or, European football's greatest individual honour, which had been announced just a fortnight earlier. In between the two extremes of the Welshman's career – the spindly speedster and the midfield puppeteer – this was the version of Giggs which had mastered the art of wingplay, while also retaining the ability to seamlessly transfer his talents to central areas.

As opponents continued to suffer at his hands, Bradford's Andy O'Brien suffered more than most. The Republic of Ireland defender was terrorised all afternoon as the Bantams clung to parity at Valley Parade but, soon after Teddy Sheringham's late opener, O'Brien was subjected to a harrowing episode at Giggs's mercy. Mikael Silvestre's long ball was bridled by the Welshman's silken control, allowing him to sprint at O'Brien, drag him infield and turn him outfield before smashing a low finish past Gary Walsh.

Ryan was soon voted the third-greatest player in United's history by readers of the club's official magazine, which marked its 100th issue in January 2001. Only George Best and Eric Cantona finished ahead of the Welshman, and the second-placed Ulsterman paid handsome tribute to the Reds' current No. 11. 'I knew Ryan was going to have success because of the quality of player he was,' said Best. 'But I don't think anyone could have imagined the level of success.'

Even by mid-January, Giggs's seventh title appeared a foregone conclusion and, after an early FA Cup exit at the hands of West Ham, the Champions League once again took centre stage for the winger and his colleagues. Having successfully navigated the second group stage, however, the Reds would once again exit at the quarter-final hurdle as Bayern Munich exacted a modicum of revenge for their 1999 suffering.

Ryan flashes the ball past Bradford City's former United goalkeeper Gary Walsh.

Celebrating a seventh Premier League title alongside teammate and PFA Player of the Year, Teddy Sheringham.

recruited to oversee Keane's rehabilitation from a knee injury – worked with Giggs on an almost daily basis as he sought to banish his issues once and for all.

'When I was working with Roy at first, Ryan was always one of the players hanging around in the background, assessing what was happening,' he said. 'Very quickly, he decided that he wanted to join in, so he was very inquisitive as to what every exercise was and how it was going to help him. Whether it was boxing, weightlifting, stretching ... he was into it. He really liked being in the gym and we spent a lot of time together.

'So, at the time that he decided to get to the bottom of his injuries, he came to the medical staff and myself and basically gave us a blank canvas to help him get over them. I spent a lot of time studying how to be corrective from a conditioning point of view – not a medical aspect, because the medical team at United were excellent – but I wanted to go from a different angle. I had a lot of meetings and went on a lot of courses so I could put together a programme for Ryan's hamstrings. He would be there all the time going through the programme, which is very rare. For top-end rehab for injury prevention, he was there virtually every day. Once that programme was finalised, it meshed together with the work of the medical staff and it seemed to work really well.'

The advice of the medical staff included Giggs changing his car and bed, and fine-tuning his diet. He also stepped up mid-section work to strengthen his lower back, tried acupuncture, visited an osteopath and, before long, also began an affiliation with yoga which would play a key role in his staggering longevity.

'I used to do yoga myself and I never felt it was quite right for footballers, so I did my own kind of stretching which worked for the lads,' said Clegg. 'Giggsy was the one who felt he could go further, and I told him that yoga would suit him down to the ground. He has a deep personality and he came across as somebody who could meditate, so we talked about it a lot. I discussed it with one of our physios, Neil Hough, at length and we decided to get started sourcing yoga teachers. Eventually we brought in a girl named Louise McMullan.'

For Giggs, the first encounter with the club's new yoga teacher would leave a lasting impression. 'She was doing a yoga session in the gym, I think with Gary Neville, and I wandered over and had a little chat with her,' he said. 'I said I'd had problems with my hamstrings and back, and asked if she could help me out. So I did the session a couple of days later and it was the hardest thing I've ever done. Halfway through I'm thinking: "I'm never, ever doing this ever again," because it was so hard, and she was particularly strict as well. I instantly felt the effects. Halfway through I was never ever doing it again, then I went home and slept for two hours, but I just felt brilliant. It was like I floated out of the gym, it was just so different. So I carried on doing it and my hamstring injuries became less and less. It's fair to say that yoga probably added a few years on to my career.'

Amid a time of self-assessment and change, Giggs was also compelled to consider his playing style. As long as he wanted to be an explosive, slaloming talent, his hamstrings would remain at risk, and that realisation had lasting repercussions for the Welshman. 'I began changing my playing style in my late twenties when I felt that I was starting to lose that electric speed I'd had when I was younger,' he admitted. 'In games, it wasn't getting me out of trouble like it perhaps used to. I tried to develop my game and, to be honest, I sort of lost my way a little bit. I didn't know what I was. Was I a flying winger? Or was I somebody who passed the ball, manoeuvred the ball a little bit more? I think my form suffered for maybe a year or so while I found out which sort of player I wanted to be.'

That search for identity and form straddled the end of the 2001-02 campaign and the start of the following term, yet there would be occasional outings of brilliance – particularly both legs of a Champions League quarter-final tie against Deportivo La Coruna. 'Giggs caused us the most trouble,' muttered Depor coach Javier Irureta, after the Welshman terrorised his side in a support-striker's role. 'It's very difficult to play two direct strikers in European competition,' Ferguson admitted. 'I decided to have Ryan behind Ruud because I know he's got courage and got great pace. He made it very difficult for Deportivo and, to be successful in Europe, you have to attack.'

While Giggs had an effort cleared off the line in a 2-0 first-leg win at the Riazor, he did find the net when the sides reconvened at Old Trafford, meandering in from the right wing and scoring a sensational solo goal to wrap up a 5-2 aggregate victory against the fancied Spaniards. That was the end of the road, however, with Bayer Leverkusen denying United and Ferguson a dream final against Real Madrid in Glasgow, while Arsenal wrested the Premier League title back to Highbury as the Reds finished third – outside the top two for the first time in a decade.

Bolstered by the big-money recruitment of Rio Ferdinand, the Reds clearly meant business in their bid to rescale the heights of European competition, and Giggs's form in the opening weeks of 2002-03 promised to aid the pursuit of that aim. He was especially clinical in front of goal, firing in impressive finishes at Chelsea, Sunderland and Charlton, while also heading home the first goal of the Reds' campaign in the Champions League proper, against Maccabi Haifa.

Irony would soon strike, however. Giggs's concoction of a new regime to reduce the risk of suffering injuries ensured that he was invariably available to his manager. With knocks, strains and illness depriving Ferguson of several other important players, Ryan was suddenly playing every week for the first time in almost a decade, and captaining the side in Keane's stead. The absence of injury deprived him of the sporadic breaks which had allowed him to catch his breath midway through campaigns, and his form slumped as a result.

United toiled towards the turn of the year, suffering defeats at Blackburn and Middlesbrough which allowed champions Arsenal to

Another outstanding European display, this time at Deportivo La Coruna, but Ryan is denied by the woodwork despite beating goalkeeper Francisco Molina.

A run of sub-standard form culminates in a poor performance against Blackburn in which Giggs comes in for criticism from a section of the home support at Old Trafford.

he backpedalled towards the travelling supporters. A timely reminder of who he was and what he could do.

Such notice was repeatedly served over the remainder of the season. Fully fit, despite his early withdrawal in Turin, the winger would appear in all 15 remaining games, starting 14, as United began to make inroads into Arsenal's longstanding advantage. While van Nistelrooy and Scholes shared the majority of the goals and Beckham found himself in the spotlight for both his plentiful assists and growing rumours of a move to Real Madrid, Giggs's return to form garnered little attention yet was key to wresting the title back from Highbury.

A sublime cross from the left winger allowed Beckham to score the only goal at Villa Park, while he also assisted van Nistelrooy for his hat-trick goal against Fulham and Solskjaer for the fourth goal in a satisfying stroll against Liverpool. Giggs also got on the scoresheet against Gerard Houllier's side, prodding home his first Premier League goal at Old Trafford for almost two full years, and he also scored and assisted in the 6-2 romp at Newcastle, providing Solskjaer's vital equaliser before smashing in the Reds' fourth of the afternoon.

Four days later, he was at it again, releasing van Nistelrooy to break the deadlock in a pivotal meeting with the Gunners and then, after Thierry Henry's scruffy double had United in peril, it was Giggs who met Solskjaer's cross to nod home a priceless equaliser. The challengers maintained a three-point advantage with just four games to go, and Arsene Wenger's shaken side would soon crumble under United's incessant pressure.

While assists and heavy involvement in three goals across the two legs of a thrilling 5-6 aggregate defeat to Real Madrid couldn't rescue United's Champions League campaign, Giggs's influence on the title race remained indispensable. Arsenal's slip at Bolton opened the door for the Reds to forge ahead, and it was Giggs who provided a sublime cross for Scholes to score a late opener at Tottenham on a key weekend. That assist – which also followed a slaloming run against

One for the doubters. Ryan requires just 40 minutes of action at Juventus to score twice, including this superb solo goal, complete with a right-foot finish.

After two years without a goal at Old Trafford, Giggs's prodded finish against Liverpool provokes glee galore among his teammates.

brought to the club and now it's down to them to show everyone what they've got.'

While Howard caught the eye with a series of fine early-season displays to usurp goalkeeper Fabien Barthez, it was Ronaldo's start to life at Old Trafford that ignited imaginations. Bolton Wanderers visited Old Trafford on the opening day of the season and fell behind when Giggs curled home an exquisite first-half free-kick – his first such goal since August 1993, almost exactly a decade earlier – but the Welshman's thunder was soon stolen.

'Ryan Giggs's bid to be the new David Beckham lasted precisely an hour,' noted Paul Wilson, of the *Guardian*. 'The Welshman's clean strike from a 30-yard free-kick looked like being the only talking point of a drab opening match until Sir Alex Ferguson introduced 18-year-old Cristiano Ronaldo to enliven proceedings. The coltish Portugal player certainly did that. Manchester United blew away Bolton Wanderers with three goals in the last half-hour and could have had more. No one was talking about Beckham at the end of the match and not even a second goal from Giggs could promote him back to top billing.'

'With Seba and Becks not here, I get a few more chances,' Giggs grinned wryly, when asked about his free-kick. The topic on everybody's mind, however, was of Ronaldo. 'I think he did very well,' said the Portuguese's left-wing counterpoint. 'There was a general buzz around the place when the fans saw him come on. Obviously they have heard a lot about him and we've seen him first-hand against Sporting Lisbon last week and, of course, in training. He's that kind of player who gets people off their seats and that's what this club is all about. You want players like that.'

The instant hype surrounding the £12.3 million signing immediately evoked memories of Giggs's own time as a teen sensation. Ferguson used those times as the template for how Ronaldo would be guided through the choppy waters of hype. 'Cristiano has

Ryan cuts a thoughtful figure during a break in a promotional photo-shoot, ahead of the 2003-04 campaign in which he would take on more seniority and responsibility.

the persistent hamstring problems which dogged me for many years, now seem to have cleared up dramatically,' he admitted. 'I don't want to jinx it, but it's true that they've not given me any real problems for almost two years. It's great to be injury-free but, touch wood, that's how it will stay!'

Stuttgart found the winger in fine fettle, embellishing a neat assist for van Nistelrooy with a clinical finish when sent clear by the Dutchman. But while progress in Europe and a three-point lead at the head of the Premier League represented a promising first half of the season, the suspension of Rio Ferdinand for missing a drugs test would derail the Reds' campaign in both leading competitions.

Dropped points against mid-table or struggling opponents such as Wolverhampton Wanderers, Middlesbrough, Leeds United, Fulham and Manchester City allowed Arsenal to run away with the title race, while Jose Mourinho was catapulted into English football's consciousness with his Porto side's controversial second-round win to end the Reds' tilt at the Champions League.

Only the FA Cup remained in United's sights and, though Arsene Wenger's league leaders awaited in the semi-finals, Ferguson's men were able to muster one last gargantuan effort to upset the odds. Once again, Giggs would torment the Gunners at Villa Park as provider for Paul Scholes. Five years earlier, the Welshman had ignored his colleague's demands of a cross in favour of scoring his greatest goal but, on this occasion, he squared for Scholes to thunder home the only goal of an unforgettable afternoon.

The Gunners' procession to replace United as champions prompted a collective slump in form thereafter, winning just two of the final six league games, but Giggs saw a return to Cardiff for the looming FA Cup final clash with Millwall as an ideal means of overcoming a largely underwhelming campaign of transition.

'If we can win the FA Cup, it would be a great end to a disappointing season and give us fresh impetus going into the next

On the rampage against Arsenal full-back Lauren – one of his pricklier adversaries – as the Reds triumph over the Gunners at Villa Park once again.

133

campaign,' he said. 'When you don't win the title at United, there are always questions asked, tough questions. We had the same scenario last season when we were going through another bad patch and the same questions were being raised. But it's all about what you do when the chips are down.'

Millwall duly found out, succumbing meekly to a 3-0 defeat in which Giggs teed up two goals for van Nistelrooy, winning a second-half penalty and drilling in a cross for the Dutchman to jab home the final goal of a routine afternoon. Though Ronaldo once again took the plaudits for a superb display headlined by the opening goal, the contribution of the man on the opposite flank had been just as vital to United's success.

Giggs's fourth FA Cup winners' medal would prove to be his last, a full decade before his retirement. In the intervening seasons, however, it looked for two seasons that cup finals and silverware would become a rarity as the Premier League's established order was violently shaken up. Chelsea had elbowed their way into the top two at United's expense, but set about ascending further with the appointment of Mourinho as manager and an extravagant spending spree from club owner Roman Abramovich.

United also spent handsomely, bringing in England sensation Wayne Rooney, Argentine defender Gabriel Heinze, Ireland's Liam Miller and, unlikeliest of all, Leeds United's emblematic striker Alan Smith. While the latter smashed home the Reds' consolation goal in a Community Shield defeat to champions Arsenal, it was Giggs who notched the first meaningful goal of the season, levelling up with a calm finish after United had fallen behind at Dynamo Bucharest.

A 2-1 first-leg win in Romania preceded a lacklustre defeat to Mourinho's Chelsea as the Premier League term opened in frustrating fashion. Giggs was heavily involved in both goals as Norwich were overcome for the Reds' first win of the domestic season, but his presence was deemed unnecessary as Bucharest were comfortably

Winning the FA Cup for the fourth and final time, Giggs enjoys the moment with Paul Scholes.

seen off in Manchester. Assists were the winger's chief currency in the opening weeks of the campaign, with his set-pieces responsible for Heinze's debut goal at Bolton and both parts of a Mikael Silvestre double against Liverpool.

When Giggs's first goal of the season arrived at the end of September, it was sensationally overshadowed. The Welshman's fine, glanced header against Fenerbahce at Old Trafford was soon forgotten as Rooney became only the second player in United's history to score a debut hat-trick, not that the fuss was allowed to pervade the home dressing room afterwards. 'He was buzzing,' recalled Giggs. 'But the older lads, myself included, did our best not to let him get too carried away, and the gaffer certainly didn't make a fuss of him. He said: "Well done, great goals," but that was it.'

Despite the addition of England's boy wonder, United's predicted surge failed to materialise. The next victory arrived four games later, at the expense of Arsene Wenger's 'Invincible' Arsenal team, who were bidding to reach 50 Premier League games without defeat. A hard-fought 2-0 win for the Reds was instantly negated by the subsequent game's loss at Portsmouth, in which an off-colour performance from Giggs prompted his removal from the team for four games in early November.

'The reaction Sir Alex got was probably the one he wanted,' Ryan explained. 'When I got back in the side, I made sure he couldn't leave me out again!' The Welshman, who turned thirty-one that month, scored on his return against Charlton and impressed over the Christmas period, notching thrice more against Bolton, Aston Villa and Middlesbrough. Nevertheless, Giggs's future was coming under scrutiny among members of the media, who became aware that he and United had not agreed the terms of the player's next contract, owing to the club's policy of only offering one-year extensions to players aged thirty or over.

After his devastating display at Boro's Riverside Stadium, Giggs drew a resounding salute from defender Rio Ferdinand. 'Gary Neville

Cristiano Ronaldo emerged as a new kid on the block and learned from the best.

Another flashpoint in a typically feisty clash with Arsenal. Here, Jens Lehmann takes issue with Ryan and his colleagues as the Gunners' long unbeaten run comes to a close.

said the other day that you shouldn't have to justify the importance of Ryan Giggs to this football club and I would echo that,' said the defender. 'He shouldn't have to justify himself. He is probably the most decorated player in English football. He is still doing it as well as ever. For anyone to doubt his ability makes you laugh. I certainly wouldn't let him go. I am sure every other player in the team would echo that. I don't think he will be going anywhere.'

Ferdinand's words would ultimately prove prescient, but in the intervening period the squad's collective focus was on extending an impressive run of league form. Keeping pace with Chelsea was a borderline impossibility, however, and Mourinho's side exerted their authority over Ferguson's men in the League Cup semi-finals, despite a wonderfully crafty lob by Giggs to briefly level the tie at Old Trafford. 'That is sublime,' cooed ITV's Peter Drury. 'Magic. Just magic. One gloriously subtle touch with the left slipper of Ryan Giggs and Manchester United are level.' Damien Duff's late free-kick sent the Blues through to Wembley, and Mourinho's men were so far ahead of the chasing pack that the February meeting between United and Arsenal – trailing by 11 and 10 points respectively – would, for once, have little bearing on the title race. Not that the spectacle suffered.

In a game preceded by a pre-match altercation between Keane and Patrick Vieira, Giggs played a starring role. The Premier League's Dubious Goals Panel cruelly deprived him of the Reds' first-half equaliser, a low shot which deflected off Ashley Cole, but there was no mistaking his role in setting up two goals for Ronaldo. The second, a fleet-footed surge past goalkeeper Manuel Almunia and right-footed cross from the most unforgiving of angles, was sensational.

On a lesser scale, so too was his cameo at Manchester City 12 days later. Fearful of damaging his hamstrings in inclement weather, Giggs opted to sport support tights and only made the decision public when he stripped to join the fray as a second-half substitute, to the amusement of a packed City of Manchester Stadium. 'I was coming

Giggs's sublime goal against Chelsea in the 2005 League Cup semi-final, second leg ultimately counted for nothing.

who would occupy the wide positions, while Fletcher would bolster central midfield to help overpower the Gunners. Beaten home and away by the Reds in the Premier League, plus a League Cup fifth-round tie, Arsene Wenger opted for a defensive approach and watched on as his side were dominated throughout a rain-soaked affair at Cardiff's Millennium Stadium.

By the time Giggs was introduced for the start of extra time, the deposed champions had been battered but somehow avoided conceding as Ferguson's side found either goalkeeper Jens Lehmann or the woodwork in their way as a procession of chances came and went begging. In a cruel end to a trying season, the Reds suffered a 5-4 defeat on penalties after Lehmann saved from Scholes. For only the second time in seven years, United ended the campaign without any silverware to show for their efforts.

The post-match end-of-season gathering was, predictably, a blend of disappointment and mystification. 'Everybody kept telling one another: "Right, we'll forget it and have a good night," but in those circumstances you go from banter and forced laughter to awkward silence and then: "How the hell did we lose that game?" You try to enjoy yourself, but the result keeps coming back to you,' Giggs admitted.

There would be some semblance of compensation for the veteran star with the agreement of a new, two-year contract, while United were further boosted by the summer acquisitions of Edwin van der Sar and Ji-sung Park. While the latter earned the man of the match award on his full debut at Everton, it was the former whose influence was most noticeable, notching clean sheets in seven of his first eight games as the Reds set off at a pace designed to ask questions of defending champions Chelsea.

For Giggs, the opening weeks of the campaign were largely a watching brief as Ferguson explored his formational options, trialling Park in wide areas, dropping Kieran Richardson into the team and also experimenting with a 4-3-3 set-up. Only in the Champions League

New boy Ji-sung Park watches on as Ryan limbers up for training at Carrington.

was Ryan a first-team fixture, notching his first goal of the season with a deflected free-kick in a 2-1 victory over Benfica. Incredibly, United would score just once more in their five remaining group games as a strong start to the term fizzled out amid a spate of injuries which, most notably, claimed Keane with a broken foot.

The Irishman, who joined Heinze, Gary Neville, Wes Brown, Louis Saha and Quinton Fortune on the sidelines, continued to make headlines during his absence with a no-nonsense assessment of his team-mates' display in a humiliating 4-1 defeat at Middlesbrough. 'More than any other player I've seen, he affects players around him,' was Giggs's verdict on his inspirational skipper, but Keane's 12-year Old Trafford career came to an end in November 2005 when his contract was cancelled. The ramifications for Giggs would emerge later in the season, but at the time of the shock announcement, the Welshman had also joined United's walking wounded.

Captain for the occasion of his 100th European outing for United, as Lille arrived at Old Trafford, the winger turned in a lively display, hitting a post with a free-kick and looking the likeliest to pierce the visitors' stubborn defensive wall. Then, he sustained a serious facial injury in an aerial collision with French midfielder Mathieu Bodmer and was forced to play on when referee Stefano Farina refused to allow physiotherapist Rob Swire on to the field.

'Ryan has three fractures in his cheekbone, that's going to be plated in his operation,' Ferguson said. 'That will keep him out for quite a spell, but the fortunate thing is that nothing serious happened while he was on the pitch. I couldn't believe it; you could see the indentation on his face. By playing on, if he had got another blow he could have got terrible eye damage.

'If our physio had been allowed to go on the pitch, he would have seen the extent of the injury and brought him off but he played on for 20 minutes. I don't know why the referee wouldn't let him on; the physio was certainly trying to get on. It was an elbow that did it

Ryan captained the team against Lille in his 100th European appearance.

But the occasion was marred by a serious facial injury that required surgery.

and we are looking at the thing at the moment. We are assessing the situation.'

The setback made for a mixed few days for Giggs, whose long-term contribution to his craft resulted in his induction to the English Football Hall of Fame, joining United colleagues past and present like Ferguson, Keane, Bryan Robson, Eric Cantona and Peter Schmeichel, as well as all-time club legends Sir Matt Busby, Duncan Edwards, Sir Bobby Charlton, Denis Law and George Best.

By the time of his return, United's season of tumult had continued. Not only had Keane departed, the club was mourning the death of Best. Giggs's early comparisons with the Ulsterman had forged a bond between the two, who shared interviews for the club magazine and even released an official video together. They remained respectful of each other's talents to the end, with Best admitting: 'Ryan gets me on the edge of my seat when he runs at defenders. As soon as he gets the ball, he goes at players. He gets better and better.'

On the field, the biggest jolt of the campaign came less than a fortnight after Best's passing, at the scene of one of his greatest displays: Benfica's Stadium of Light. United had failed to score in all four group games against Lille and Villarreal, and required a positive result to limp into the knockout stages of the competition. Despite Scholes' early opener, the hosts hit back to secure a 2-1 victory and Ferguson's men exited an apparently navigable group with just six points and three goals scored. Before a backdrop of ongoing domestic toil – Chelsea already had a ten-point lead over the second-placed Reds – Ferguson and United came under staggering scrutiny.

*The Times*'s Jonathan Northcroft, who labelled Giggs 'one of the few left in United's ranks who knows what being good enough entails', cast doubt over the manager's future, opining: 'The great man is entitled to go out any way he likes. But it seems increasingly that go he must.' The view was widespread across the press, with the *Irish Times*'s Richard Williams speculating: 'His new target will be to ensure that the closing months of a glorious era do not leave Gary Neville, Ryan Giggs and Paul Scholes without a final trophy to mark the passing of United's golden generation.'

Far calmer was the mood within the camp. 'We just haven't been good enough,' admitted Giggs, who fronted up to face the press post-match. 'I think everyone has to take responsibility for the Benfica result. The results don't lie; we had too many draws, even in a tight group. We had the perfect start against Benfica, it was disappointing to concede two quick goals after that, but we still had plenty of time to do something about it. We should have defended better as a team after going 1-0 ahead. We went for that second goal which, looking back, we shouldn't have done.'

In the side's next outing, a home league game against Everton, it was down to the timeless brilliance of Giggs and Scholes to demonstrate their enduring value to the cause. Trailing early in the first period, the Reds were hauled level by a spark of old-school genius as Scholes's long-range pass fell perfectly into Giggs's path, the onrushing Welshman demonstrated his silken touch with a deft, first-time finish past Richard Wright, before embarking on animated celebrations in front of Old Trafford's Scoreboard End.

Soon enough, Scholes would join the list of injury absentees as he succumbed to a mysterious and worrying eye injury. Fletcher would join him in the short term, while an horrendous broken and dislocated ankle suffered at Anfield would rule makeshift midfielder Smith out for over a year. Still searching for the answer to the Keane conundrum, Ferguson even repurposed Ferdinand and Rooney into an unlikely pairing without success, before settling on perhaps an even more improbable axis for the League Cup final meeting with Wigan Athletic.

Giggs partnered versatile defender John O'Shea in Cardiff, and they shone despite their collective experience of the role being limited to Ryan's occasional central deployment in major European ties in the mid- to late-1990s. 'I am comfortable there,' he stressed. 'In midfield, they are not used

to people running at them as the full-backs are. You can have a bigger impact on the game.' O'Shea, for his part, grinned: 'Giggsy makes it easy for me. Obviously he's performed the role before and he's good enough to do it when required. I really enjoy playing there with him – I'm happy to play wherever the club wants me – so let's see where it takes us.'

'Giggsy makes it easy for me. Obviously he's performed the [midfield] role before and he's good enough to do it when required. I really enjoy playing there with him.'

**John O'Shea**
Manchester United

In the short-term, the move had secured the first piece of silverware for many of Giggs's junior peers, while over the remaining months of the campaign it allowed the Reds to end the season on the crest of a wave. Following victory in Cardiff, the Giggs-O'Shea axis began 11 of the final 12 league games and won nine. Though Chelsea again strolled to the title, clinching it with a painfully one-sided win over United at Stamford Bridge, the Reds' end-of-season haul of 83 points was more than respectable. But, while it beat the Treble season's winning total by four points, it was only enough to register a second-place finish in 2005-06.

Nevertheless, in a campaign of such sustained upheaval, with injuries, controversies, changes of formation and club ownership all conspiring to distract at the same time as Chelsea continued to grow in stature, the disappointment didn't linger too long. News of United's demise had been greatly exaggerated, and Ferguson knew it.

On opposite sides in training, Ryan and John O'Shea would soon form an unlikely central midfield alliance.

'We don't want to be playing catch-up,' warned Ryan who, at thirty-two, turned back the clock and produced decisive interventions in the opening fixtures. 'Chelsea have the ability to buy who they want and their consistency in the last two years has meant no one has touched them.'

Although proud to be often wearing the captain's armband in the absence of long-term injury victim Gary Neville, stressing he was only keeping it warm for the right-back, it led to regular media commitments which he took effortlessly in his stride. This was nothing, however, compared to how he was performing on the field.

A pinpoint cross set up Louis Saha in a 5-1 opening-weekend thrashing of Fulham and he joined the Frenchman in attack during the 3-0 win at Charlton Athletic. After hitting the woodwork with a free-kick at The Valley, he marked his 600th start for the club with a coolly taken winner at Watford, rounding Richard Lee to slip home, prompting MUTV's Paddy Crerand to purr: 'He is playing like he did when he was seventeen, when he first came through. His fitness levels are amazing.'

Another vital contribution followed as a fourth successive win was accrued against Tottenham when August's Barclays Player of the Month (the first time he had scooped the award) headed in the rebound after Paul Robinson pushed out Cristiano Ronaldo's swerving set piece. 'I've had a long rest during the summer and maybe that has helped,' commented Ryan. 'I certainly feel fresh and as though I have hit the ground running.'

The truth is Giggs, in the words of teammate Neville, had simply matured into a 'brilliant player' and was capable of influencing games from a new central position. With a licence to roam, he was timing and selecting his runs and unlocking defences with his incisive approach work. Whether out on the left or in the middle, he was in exceptional form and a creative force to be reckoned with.

'Mainly, we see him as a central player, either in midfield or playing off the front,' stated Sir Alex. 'For fifteen years or so, he'd been

On the scoresheet and playing as well as ever, Ryan starts the 2006-07 season with a bang and the winner at Watford.

Proudly showing off a first Barclays Player of the Month award alongside top boss Sir Alex Ferguson.

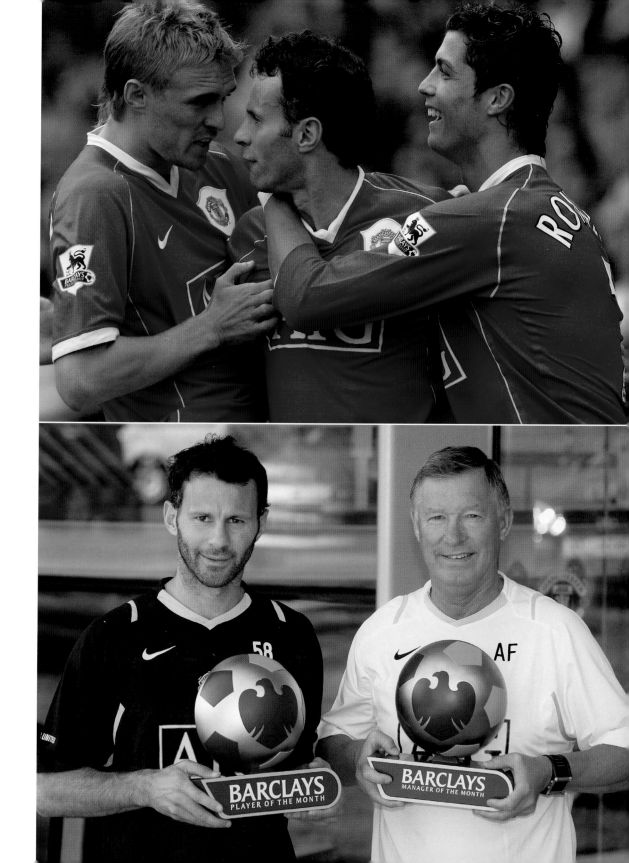

tramping up and down that touchline and there is no player in the Premier League that can do that or has done that. They've all either died, been shoved aside or folded! But he's been amazing in terms of having the capacity to keep wanting to do it.'

Just when everything was going to plan, the hamstring curse struck again as he was injured when earning a penalty in a Champions League victory over Celtic. It was his right leg rather than the left that had caused so many previous issues. United sensibly did not rush him back, and the player was learning how to manage such problems, so he missed a month as the Reds dropped points. A timely return followed at Wigan Athletic when he came off the bench for Wes Brown at the interval and set up the equaliser, Nemanja Vidic's first goal for the club, en route to a 3-1 triumph.

Giggs had a key role in both goals during the pleasing success against Liverpool at Old Trafford, excelled during a much-lauded team performance against Bolton Wanderers and crossed for Saha to claim a priceless winner at Blackburn Rovers as United kept their noses in front of Chelsea at the summit. His assists were becoming a regular occurrence as Sir Alex's men opened up a six-point lead by the turn of the year, while a key contribution in the crucial Champions League tie with Benfica – providing the set piece for Vidic's equaliser and then soaring to head home the clinching goal himself – ensured qualification for the knockout stages.

Giggs added to his tally with the final strike in the remarkable 4-0 thumping of Tottenham at White Hart Lane in early February, slamming past Robinson to net in the season's second fixture against Spurs, one of his favourite opponents. Even though his 80th-minute replacement, John O'Shea, was forced to go in goal for the final ten minutes when Edwin van der Sar broke his nose, the Reds still kept a clean sheet and were looking genuine title favourites.

The manager was still cautious but forecast the value Giggs, Neville and Paul Scholes would provide come the period of the season

Benfica have no answer to Ryan's trickery at Old Trafford.

Enjoying a piece of quick-thinking that upset Lille in the Champions League. Paul Scholes and Wayne Rooney approve of his impudence.

giant, Roma, in the previous round, with a 7-1 second-leg scoreline at Old Trafford stunning the football world. Giggs, like so many of his colleagues, was sensational and had a hand in four of the goals. 'Ryan has deserved nights like this,' suggested Sir Alex. 'He rises to it.' It was also his inviting through ball that led to Rooney's winner in first leg against Milan. However, defending the 3-2 lead with tired legs proved an impossible task and a 0-3 reverse was a bitter pill to swallow.

At least the priority mission – ending Chelsea's domestic dominance – was completed as planned. While the three points at Manchester City were secured only by a late penalty save by van der Sar, they proved sufficient to wrap up the title when Chelsea were held to a 1-1 draw by Arsenal. Giggs watched the London derby at a friend's house and celebrated with his United-supporting mates after pacing his way through the 90 minutes. He had grown so agitated a couple of weeks earlier that he had switched off Chelsea's clash with Newcastle at the same house, but felt the 0-0 scoreline on Tyneside made the venue a lucky one.

There were two games to spare, including what turned out to be a goalless affair at Stamford Bridge, with Sir Alex fielding a shadow side that received a guard of honour from the deposed champions. The shrewd Scot was mindful not to give away too many clues ahead of another meeting with Mourinho's men in the first FA Cup final back at the rebuilt Wembley.

Even a shock loss to West Ham on the final day of the league season could not dampen the celebrations, although many Reds (and probably Giggs, too) would have lost little sleep in relegating a team that had caused so much pain at this stage of the season in the first half of the 1990s. There was still a sense that United were not firing on all cylinders ahead of the FA Cup final, which would provide Mourinho with ample opportunity for some form of revenge in front of a global audience. Giggs was chosen to lead the team out in his latest quest for another winner's medal. 'Ryan will be captain,' confirmed Sir Alex beforehand.

In a game best remembered for Cristiano Ronaldo's late winner, Ryan brilliantly skews home one of the goals of his career at Fulham.

Although outnumbered on this occasion, Ryan and United mounted an incredible comeback at Everton to take a huge step towards a first title in four seasons.

in the camp was relaxed, with Ryan joking to Ronaldo, who had a reputation for going to ground easily, that he was still the expert at winning spot-kicks, even if it was a stone-waller. 'Ryan was made for this football club and has given a lot to it,' said the Portugal superstar.

Arsenal were usurped as leaders by Boxing Day, only for another surprise defeat at West Ham to generate a shock to the system, even though Giggs crossed for Ronaldo to head the first goal. The answer to adversity? Winning all six games in January with only one goal conceded, including a six-goal slaughter of Newcastle United when Ronaldo's hat-trick naturally overshadowed another Giggs assist for Tevez.

Ryan, by now an MBE after earning a spot on the Queen's birthday honours list, proudly donned the captain's armband for the derby with Manchester City that marked the fiftieth anniversary of the Munich disaster and it was a poignant spectacle with both clubs wearing classic strips, shorn of badges and sponsorship logos. The sombre, reflective occasion affected the Reds, who slipped five points behind Arsenal after a 1-2 defeat, but the champions were back on top of the table by the time Ryan returned to the side for a nervous 1-0 success at Derby.

He had also appeared in Lyon, skippering the team in his 100th Champions League outing, when Tevez continued his happy knack of notching vital late goals, but the Welshman was being used more sparingly at this stage by his manager. 'For me, Ryan has been an absolute model in his time with us,' Sir Alex stated. 'Even at thirty-four, we expect big, big things of him. Obviously, we don't play him in every game, but that's natural for someone of that age. We want to play him in the games that really, really matter to our football club.

'Throughout his time with us, Ryan has always reserved his best performances for the biggest occasions. I've said many times about occasions at Old Trafford and the atmosphere and the great nights we've had there. They could only happen because the right type of players are playing on that stage and Ryan has produced many great moments for us.'

A December downpour against Derby County cannot dampen the joy of claiming a 100th league goal for the club.

A poignant occasion as the Manchester derby marks the 50th anniversary of the Munich disaster. Ryan and opposite number Richard Dunne lead the teams out behind Sven-Goran Eriksson and Sir Alex.

to cover most of it. But, in practice, Ryan had found the same corner nine times out of ten and admitted to being 'quite confident'. His aim was true and the ball had the net billowing as the Czech Republic international dived the wrong way. 'Come on!' he roared to the fans that had made the long trip and were experiencing the full gamut of emotions as the night drew ever longer in the Russian capital.

The next penalty, by Nicolas Anelka, was palmed away by van der Sar and history was made. Giggs lifted the trophy with captain Rio Ferdinand and the sense of fulfilment must have been overwhelming. 'I think it is fate,' he gasped. 'We could not have planned it any better.'

Sir Alex suggested Ferdinand lift the European Cup with the substitute. 'I said to Rio would you mind if Ryan lifted the trophy and he said: "Absolutely not." Ryan said: "No, Rio is captain. He should be going." But we said: "Ryan, you deserve to take the trophy."' It would never be an issue with Ferdinand to share the magical experience, as it wasn't for Neville when the title was won a year earlier. 'Lifting the cup with Giggsy was a great moment for me,' insisted the centre-back. 'He's a living legend, somebody who probably is not appreciated as much as he should be.'

Ronaldo was the star of the side, a true world-class talent, but Giggs was the player most respected by his colleagues. While Ronaldo fanned the flames of speculation over his future within minutes of the final whistle, his more decorated teammate received a commemorative watch during the celebrations back at the hotel.

'Oh, he is god in there [the dressing room],' recalled Sir Alex. 'Absolutely. The reaction he got from the players after the final, when they made a presentation at the reception ... it was a fantastic moment. They started to sing his song and he really was emotional about it. The players were great with him and he deserved it. You can see the warmth he generates in the dressing room.'

Chief executive David Gill was another privileged to be present to witness the special moment. 'I think it was very emotional coming

Buried under his grateful colleagues, the evergreen Welshman has clinched another league title – his tenth – with a calmly taken goal at Wigan Athletic.

Unflustered by the imposing sight of Petr Cech in the Chelsea goal, Ryan converts his Champions League final spot-kick in Moscow.

▼
Lifting Europe's grandest prize for a second time with Rio Ferdinand on a long, but unforgettable night, in the Russian capital.

keep it going." That is why the club gets stronger and stronger. We always think we can achieve more. Look at Ryan: I'm sure he sees the Premier League as his trophy and why shouldn't he? He has won it so many times it's as if he lends it out for the odd year.'

While the stage was set in the eyes of some for Giggs to call time on his career at the very top, in possession of the Champions League, Premier League and all-time club appearances record, he set about underlining his vision of a playing future with an impressive start to the following term. Having converted his penalty in a Community Shield shoot-out win over Portsmouth, Ryan then teed up Fletcher to secure a point against Newcastle on the opening day of the Premier League season. His involvement soon became sporadic, however, as Sir Alex Ferguson sought to encourage the development of Nani and Anderson in their second season, with the duo occupying left-wing and central midfield berths respectively.

Their Welsh colleague was still involved, appearing regularly from the bench, and starting and scoring in the League Cup victory over Middlesbrough, but he didn't begin successive games until mid-February, by which point he had been dipped in and out of roles on the flank and in the middle. Starts were followed by substitute outings or regular rests but, rather than be frustrated by his inconsistent involvement, Giggs was actually at the heart of planning his schedule. In accord with Ferguson, the club's coaching staff, fitness and medical departments, he embarked on a tailor-made training and recovery schedule which was fluid enough to adapt to external variables such as fixture changes or injuries to other players.

'You have to accept that, when you hit a threshold like Ryan, it takes you longer to recover from games,' said Tony Strudwick, United's Head of Fitness, in 2012. 'Ryan spends longer in recovery than the average twenty-one or twenty-two-year-old. That's just common sense. With the way the coaching department and

Ryan sparkles in the League Cup tie with Middlesbrough, skipping past defender David Wheater.

Head of Fitness Tony Strudwick keeps Giggs and the rest of the players in check.

Giggs's fears proved well founded as back-to-back defeats to Liverpool and Fulham jolted an apparent procession into a frantic scramble for the finish line. Normal service was resumed in typically terrifying fashion, as Giggs notched two assists in a priceless 3-2 victory over Aston Villa, which included the Welshman teeing up Federico Macheda's famous debut winner in injury time. Though hopes of a domestic clean sweep were ended when a much-changed Reds side were beaten on penalties by Everton in the FA Cup semi-final, Liverpool's challenge was gradually seen off. Giggs, a model of consistency while in devastatingly functional form, scored the opening goal and shone at Middlesbrough, after which Boro boss Gareth Southgate admitted: 'For any youngster playing against Giggs and Scholes, it's not just what they do on the field but the way they've lived their lives at the top of the game. They're shining examples of how to let your football do the talking.'

There would be more than words to reward Giggs's continued excellence. For weeks, with the PFA Player of the Year awards looming large, murmurs had grown citing the Welshman as a surprise contender for the honour. 'Giggs is so far ahead of the field for Footballer of the Year, he makes Master Minded look like a Cheltenham non-runner,' opined Jim White, of the *Daily Telegraph*. 'The fact is, at thirty-five, Giggs appears to be at the peak of his powers.'

Sure enough, a staggering 17 seasons after picking up his first PFA Young Player of the Year award, Giggs landed the main prize. 'It's right up there,' he beamed. 'With personal accolades, it's the best to have as it's voted by your fellow players. I've been fortunate to win a lot of trophies, I won the Young Player award twice but this is the big one.'

While Ryan was briefly elevated on an individual basis, United collectively found composure and dead-eyed form as the major team honours hoved into view. The Premier League was wrapped up with a game to spare, secured by a goalless draw at home to Arsenal, who were emphatically ousted from the Champions League at the semi-final stage. Having battered the Gunners 4-1 on aggregate, the Reds booked a final date with Barcelona in Rome. Giggs – who appeared from the bench in both semi-final games – was thrust into a starting berth by the suspension meted out to Fletcher for a ludicrously harsh red card suffered at the Emirates Stadium.

Presented with the chance to become the first team since AC Milan – winners in 1989 and 1990 – to retain the trophy, United began impressively. Cristiano Ronaldo was particularly prominent in what would prove to be his final appearance for the club, but the Reds never recovered from Samuel Eto'o's opening goal against the run of play and tamely slipped to a convincing 2-0 defeat.

'Giggs is so far ahead of the field for Footballer of the Year, he makes Master Minded look like a Cheltenham non-runner. The fact is, [that] at thirty-five, Giggs appears to be at the peak of his powers.'

**Jim White**
*Daily Telegraph*

'We didn't turn up,' lamented Giggs, who was among a handful of players in the United dressing room affected by illness on the day of the game. 'They turned up, they played some great football. Credit to them, they deserved it. At times, Barcelona can make you look silly because they keep the ball so well. At times we maybe chased it and didn't keep our shape as we should have. We have got no right to win every competition and league. You have got to earn the right.

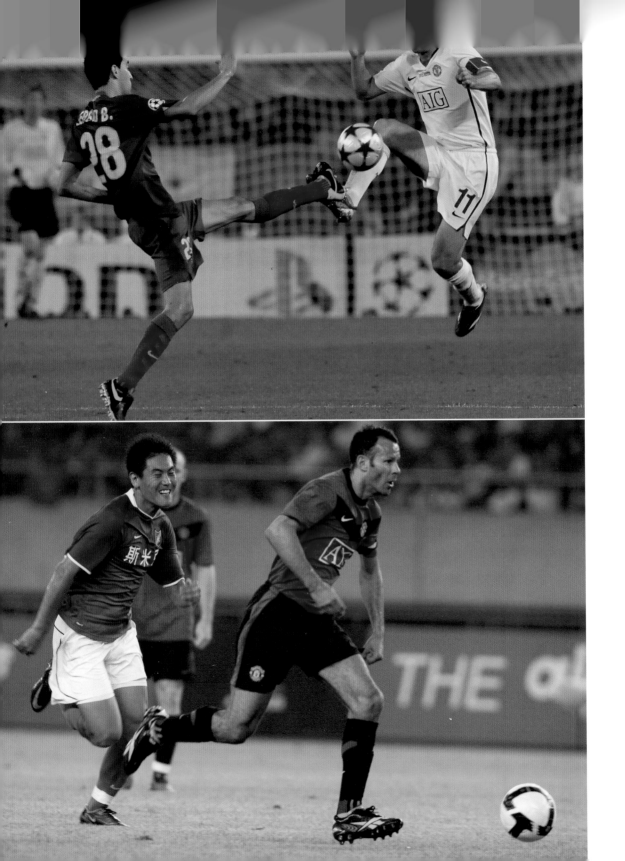

'You are on the coach outside the stadium and you know you haven't played well personally or as a team. It is the last game of the season and you'll never get it back and you are just gutted. The worst I have ever felt was my first full season when we lost the league to Leeds, but that was a close second; that feeling of emptiness.'

Despite ending the campaign with four winner's medals, it underlined Giggs's voracious appetite for success that he could end the season feeling disappointment. It replicated his feelings of the previous summer when, despite the Premier League and Champions League Double, he admitted: 'That took the shine off the season for some of us. We knew we wouldn't have a better chance of doing the Treble again.'

Though the distressing defeat in Rome was exacerbated by the loss of Ronaldo and Tevez, the show had to go on. For Giggs, that consisted of achieving a career first during the club's pre-season tour of Asia: scoring three goals in an 8-2 demolition of Hangzhou Greentown. 'I've never scored a hat-trick for United, so it was a first. Scoring goals gives you confidence ... it's certainly given me some!' beamed the Welshman, whose rich vein of form continued throughout the opening months of the 2009-10 campaign.

His first goal of the season arrived on his 700th start for the club, and it came in style as he curled a magnificent 25-yard free-kick into Carlo Cudicini's top corner in a 3-1 victory at Spurs. It would be as a provider, rather than a goalscorer, that he caught the eye thereafter, however. As Manchester City's revolution began to move through the gears – headlined by the capture of Tevez – a September meeting between the two Manchester factions at Old Trafford provided the opportunity for Giggs to stamp the Reds' authority on the fixture. After his quick throw-in led to Wayne Rooney's second-minute opener, the No. 11 duly reeled off three more direct assists, teeing up a pair of Darren Fletcher headers and summer signing Michael Owen's thrilling, last-gasp winner.

The 2008-09 Champions League final runs away from United as Sergio Busquets wins a midfield duel with Giggs in Rome.

Pre-season opponents Hangzhou Greentown are on the receiving end of Ryan's only senior hat-trick for United.

Involved in all four goals in a 4-3 victory, Giggs duly served up another pair of assists in his next outing, this time coming from the bench at Stoke City. The Reds were toiling against the pumped-up Potters until the Welshman's introduction, and he soon crossed for Dimitar Berbatov and John O'Shea to convert the winning goals.

'Halfway to seventy and still giving his opponents twisted blood,' noted the *Daily Telegraph*'s Mark Ogden. 'Ryan Giggs has started more than 700 games for Manchester United but even by the standards of his youthful exuberance, his most recent performances, at an autumnal thirty-five, have been exceptional. Sir Alex Ferguson thinks it's the fear of life after football that keeps Giggs going – he should have a thought for the Welsh winger's opponents. It took the oldest player in Ferguson's matchday squad to inject a bit of enthusiasm into a flat United team, to create two goals and win the game.'

What made Giggs's form all the more impressive was that he was displaying it in his customary position as a winger. 'We've played him out wide in a few games because he's fresh at the moment,' explained Ferguson. 'It's the beginning of the season, he's got plenty of running in him and he can do a lot of damage in the wide position. But I think you'll find that as the season progresses, he'll move back into the middle of the park where he can dictate the games.'

In the interim, Giggs continued to pass full-backs and milestones apace. His 150th United goal drew him level with arch-poacher Ruud van Nistelrooy in United's all-time standings, as well as hauling the Reds back on par with Wolfsburg in an important Champions League group stage tie. For good measure, he also teed up Michael Carrick's late winner. Less than two months on, Ryan notched his 100th Premier League goal with a late free-kick against Portsmouth. Again, though, he had starred in a support role, supplying two-thirds of Wayne Rooney's hat-trick. 'His performance was magnificent and he was the key to two of my goals,' said the England striker. 'I don't know how he does it – he is unbelievable. He is one of the sharpest every

Giggs and United enjoy a fine afternoon at Tottenham's White Hart Lane as he curls in a magnificent free-kick.

A key influence on the Manchester derby, Giggs was involved in all four United goals, including a stunning pass to tee up Michael Owen's dramatic winner.

day in training and in this game, on quite a difficult pitch and in difficult weather, he puts in a performance like that. He is quite incredible.'

Pompey manager Avram Grant, meanwhile, came close to pegging the Welshman's longevity, speculating: 'I think we will still be playing against Ryan Giggs in 2015. He doesn't look thirty-six and you would never guess he was that old. He is such a great player, so clever and a real example to all others. I have so much admiration for players like Giggs and Rooney, because I like intelligent players with enthusiasm, passion, quality and so much commitment to their team.'

For his sustained excellence in support of the collective, the veteran star soon found himself again elevated on an individual basis. To his genuine amazement, having attended without any expectation of recognition, Giggs was named the BBC Sports Personality of the Year, beating reigning Formula One world champion Jenson Button and world heptathlon champion Jessica Ennis into second and third spot respectively.

'I'd just like to thank the BBC and everyone who voted for me. This is unbelievable,' grinned Ryan. 'This is a shock – as you can tell by the speech I've prepared. I've been lucky enough to win many things in my career. I've played with some great players, the greatest manager who's ever lived, and the greatest club in the world – I thought that would get a few boos – but this is up there. I grew up watching this TV programme. To be up here is unbelievable.'

The good news kept coming. Just five days later, Giggs penned a new, one-year contract extension to ensure that his Reds career would pass the twentieth anniversary of his debut. 'I am sure he will play for another two years,' said Ferguson. 'His form is fantastic at the moment and he is playing some of his best football. My intention this season was to play Ryan in central midfield. Given his age, I just thought he may be more useful in central midfield. But it's not been that way because he's shown he can still handle it as a wide player and the rest of the midfield players have been doing OK.'

The Welshman is all smiles as United swat aside Portsmouth in torrential rain at Fratton Park.

Honoured by a wider audience, the BBC Sports Personality of the Year award catches Ryan by surprise.

# Ryan Giggs
## The Man for All Seasons

Come January, as United's Premier League jostling with Chelsea and looming Champions League tie with AC Milan were put on the back-burner, Manchester City could once again attest to Giggs's devastating influence after a thrilling League Cup semi-final. Although ex-Red Tevez scored a brace to overturn the Welshman's close-range opener in the first leg at Eastlands, the Citizens were powerless to combat his input back at Old Trafford. Leading 2-1 on the night but tied 3-3 on aggregate as injury time began, United booked a berth in the final when Giggs swung in an utterly unstoppable cross which Rooney powered home from close range. 'It's all about the flight of the ball from the veteran,' cooed Sky Sports' Alan Smith. 'It's on a plate.'

Alas, Giggs would not get the opportunity to pick up his fourth League Cup winner's medal, despite playing a huge role in taking United to Wembley. Ironically, the Welshman suffered his setback against fellow finalists Aston Villa in a Premier League meeting just 18 days before their reconvention at the national stadium. Giggs's shot had earlier deflected in off compatriot James Collins to secure a 1-1 draw for ten-man United, but a collision with Villa substitute Steve Sidwell prompted the veteran's removal near the end of the game. Subsequent X-rays confirmed that he had broken his right arm, and would be sidelined for over a month.

Not only did that deny Ryan any part in the Wembley showpiece – won 2-1, courtesy of a late Rooney header – but also meant that the AC Milan double-header came too soon. Not that the Reds struggled in his absence, sending a poor Rossoneri side to a 7-2 aggregate defeat. Giggs's eventual return coincided with the nitty-gritty stage of the season, and though he teed up another own-goal, this time from Bolton's Jlloyd Samuel in a 4-0 away win, he couldn't save United from adverse results in four key games.

A bystander reduced to eight minutes per game in both legs of an away-goals exit to Bayern Munich in the Champions League quarter-finals, Giggs started a home defeat to Chelsea and a goalless draw at

Wayne Rooney benefits from a magnificent Giggs cross to head another dramatic late derby winner, this time in the League Cup.

Joy – and a sense of relief – after converting a pair of penalties against Tottenham to keep the Reds' title hopes alive.

dressing room afterwards,' said Gill. 'He was really upset and annoyed. He felt the team had let the manager down and the youngsters hadn't shown what they could do. I think it's a measure of the man. Obviously, the League Cup was fourth on our list of priorities, but he was still very annoyed to be going out of it. He didn't think it reflected well on him and the other players.'

There would soon be an upturn in personal fortunes for the veteran, however, as he played his way into form, with his contributions particularly valuable as December meandered into January. 'Once I get into a rhythm, and it's usually around Christmas time, when it starts getting a bit colder and the games are coming and probably a lot of players are going backwards, I come into a peak then so that's a massive plus for me,' he admitted. 'And the manager knows when to use me.'

The turn of the year brought telling dividends. A match-winning penalty conversion in the second minute to ensure a defeat for Kenny Dalglish on his return to management with Liverpool in the FA Cup, before Giggs steered in a magnificent finish against Birmingham in a 5-0 romp headlined by Berbatov's fine hat-trick. Most important of all, though, was a match-turning substitute cameo at Blackpool, who led the Reds by two goals at the break at a windswept Bloomfield Road. The introduction of Giggs inspired a 3-2 comeback victory for United, with the veteran supplying a wonderful assist for Chicharito's equaliser.

'United showed the collective spirit here that defines champions and they had a player, in the form of Ryan Giggs, who oozed football intelligence,' observed the *Guardian*'s Daniel Taylor. 'It was Giggs's introduction at half time that swung this game in United's favour and put in place the kind of comeback which Ferguson's men have made a speciality over the years.'

The result put United five points clear at the top of the Premier League table, with an interest remaining in the FA Cup and the Champions League. Remarkably still unbeaten since the start of the

The opening Premier League game of the campaign, versus Newcastle, yields a Giggs goal and he takes the acclaim.

A disappointing League Cup defeat at West Ham's Upton Park prompted Giggs to issue a dressing-room dressing down to his colleagues.

> 'The game's defining memory came not from the build-ups to the goals of Javier Hernandez or Park, however fine those moves were; it came with Giggs sliding in on the sluggish Frank Lampard, winning the ball and a standing ovation,'

**Henry Winter**
*Daily Telegraph*

On as a substitute, Ryan sparks a key victory at Blackpool in January 2011. Here, Javier Hernandez equalises from a fabulous Giggs through-ball.

Chicharito regularly finished off Giggs's wonderful approach work, including this key Champions League strike against Chelsea.

season, the Reds' patchy away form had yielded just three league victories outside Old Trafford. The long and proud run of invincibility was ended by struggling Wolves in February, only for morale to be quickly restored by a Manchester derby victory best remembered for Rooney's overhead kick winner, but also notable for a sublime combination between Giggs and Nani to open the scoring.

It continued to be as a provider that the Welshman, increasingly United's most penetrative attacker, earned his slot in Ferguson's team. After teeing up Chicharito's second-round decider against Marseille, Giggs assisted all three Reds goals across both legs of an absorbing quarter-final victory over Chelsea, including another for the summer signing. The Welshman's form was reciprocally enhanced by that of the Mexican, whose movement perfectly complemented Giggs's vision.

After the second leg, the *Telegraph*'s Henry Winter again saluted the contribution of United's oldest outfield player. 'The game's defining memory came not from the build-ups to the goals of Javier Hernandez or Park, however fine those moves were; it came with Giggs sliding in on the sluggish Frank Lampard, winning the ball and a standing ovation,' he wrote.

'That moment showed who had the greater appetite: Giggs at 37, playing 90 stamina-stretching minutes in central midfield, tackling and creating, the epitome of elegant determination. Remarkable. United fans chorused his name, warning the opponents that Giggs would tear them apart again. He is a national treasure, a marvellous role model and a poster boy for the career-enhancing joys of yoga. He had Chelsea tied up in knots.'

With the Blues also lagging in the title race, United's hopes of silverware remained realistic. A repeat of 1999's Treble was dashed by Manchester City's FA Cup semi-final win at Wembley, while Germany's Schalke were regarded as dangerous underdogs in the last four of the Champions League. Their star man, former Real Madrid striker Raul, relished the chance to face off against his fellow living legend.

'What we have in common is that we love this profession,' said the Spaniard. 'Football is our lives. They are great professionals who look after themselves and who train properly. For Giggs to still be playing at this level at thirty-seven years of age is incredible. He is still playing every three or four days and often in various positions – in midfield or out wide. He is still adding new things to his game and you can only admire that. Facing them again makes this match all the more special and I hope I can swap shirts at the end of the game with Ryan Giggs. It will be a great honour to have that shirt.'

The final whistle at the Veltins Arena provided the only opportunity for Raul – or any of his colleagues – to pin Ryan down long enough to exchange words. The Reds' No. 11 turned in a sublime display throughout the game, not allowing frustration to take hold as goalkeeper Manuel Neuer rebuffed a series of efforts from the Welshman's right foot and head. As the huge German stopper continued to thwart all the visitors' attackers, it was Giggs who finally broke the deadlock in the second period. United's scouts had identified that Neuer was prone to spreading himself in the same style as Reds great Peter Schmeichel, leaving him vulnerable to nutmegs.

Finally, there is a way past Schalke keeper Manuel Neuer for Ryan in the Champions League semi-final first leg.

A salute to the supporters as United take a huge step towards a 19th title by beating Chelsea at Old Trafford.

Finally given the opportunity to test the theory by Rooney's perfect through-ball, the 37-year-old obliged, and Rooney's subsequent clincher had the Reds on course for a third final in four years.

'We created enough chances to be four or five up at half time,' grinned Giggs. 'Before the game, we'd have taken 2-0 but we're slightly disappointed it was only two. I thought if we kept creating chances, one would go in and hopefully I would get one on my left foot rather than my right foot!'

Spared the rigours of clinching qualification – which his colleagues did with a 6-1 aggregate triumph – he returned to the starting line-up for the title decider against Chelsea at Old Trafford. A year earlier, the Blues' victory at Old Trafford had effectively wrested the trophy to Stamford Bridge. This time, it would be coming back the other way, with Giggs typically heavily involved. It was his astutely threaded ball which allowed Park to tee up Chicharito's first-minute opener, before Giggs crossed for Vidic to head home what proved to be the winning goal.

Requiring a point from two remaining league games, against Blackburn and Blackpool, United still contrived to make life difficult. Brett Emerton put Rovers ahead at Ewood Park, and it needed a fine through-ball from Giggs to release Chicharito to win a second-half penalty, which Rooney duly dispatched. With that, title number 19 – or 12, for Ryan – was secured, and with it a national record number of successes. 'It means a lot, especially for the older supporters who went through the 1970s and 1980s watching Liverpool win everything,' he admitted. 'Now, obviously, the tables are turned. We've done so well over the last twenty years so to overturn that sort of deficit, to get to nineteen, is special and the fans know that.'

With a route from 18 to 19 successfully plotted, the Reds' next job was to turn a haul of three Champions League titles into four. In their way stood a Barcelona team who, two years since their convincing victory in Rome, had taken their tiki-taka possession game

Sir Alex Ferguson and coach Rene Meulensteen enjoy the thrill of closing in on more glory at Old Trafford.

200

other experienced players,' said Ferguson. 'We've a young squad now and we've always given youth a chance, but we all know the value of experience.'

'I'm experienced enough to know I'm not going to start every game or even play every game,' Giggs said ahead of the start of the season. 'The thing I want to do is be effective and contribute to the team. As soon as I stop doing that, I'll finish. Hopefully, I can just contribute to the team, to the club, whether it be starting a game or coming on and using my experience in games. You want to play every game, of course, but I know I can't.'

Symbolically, Giggs's only start in August came in van der Sar's testimonial match, as he either watched from the bench or joined the fray as a substitute while the new, youthful United set a blistering pace from the off. The season's first five games yielded 23 goals, four Premier League wins and the Community Shield against a Manchester City side matching the Reds' strong start to the term and widely tipped to challenge for the title.

For Ryan, a meeting with Chelsea brought the thorny issue of age, with newly appointed Blues manager Andre Villas-Boas nearly four years his junior. 'Yes, it's slightly strange, I suppose, seeing managers younger than me,' laughed the Welshman. 'He's obviously had a successful time at Porto and Pep Guardiola is only forty so it might be a trend that is starting to happen.'

It was on the European stage that Giggs finally began his first game of the season. He took his chance to shine in Benfica's Stadium of Light, scoring a fine equaliser to set a new record as the oldest goalscorer in the history of the Champions League, aged 37 years and 289 days. He had previously claimed the record from Italian legend Filippo Inzaghi with his strike at Schalke, 104 days earlier.

His next start also yielded an appearance on the scoresheet. Michael Owen's brace had already put the Reds comfortably ahead in a League Cup tie against old enemy Leeds United, before Giggs

A superb strike at Benfica's Stadium of Light extends Ryan's record as the Champions League's oldest goalscorer.

surged infield, nutmegged Robert Snodgrass and poked home an eye-catching goal to wrap up United's progress and silence the criticism of the home fans. 'I've no idea how he does it,' laughed Ferguson.

An uncharacteristically skewed volley meant that Giggs passed up the chance to score an injury-time winner at Stoke City, as the Reds' perfect Premier League record came to an end, but he was immediately restored to the starting line-up and obliged by assisting two Danny Welbeck goals in a 3-3 draw with Basel.

For the Longsight-born youth, the experience of playing with his veteran colleague was an unashamed thrill. 'My role model has been Ryan Giggs ever since I was a young kid,' admitted the striker. 'I love the way he plays. I just thought: "Wow! I want to be Ryan Giggs." When I first trained with him, I was in disbelief. Then I got the chance to play with him. There's nothing better than playing alongside your role models. Ryan has that great desire. He still wants to win every single training match. Even if it's possession, he wants his team to have the ball most. To see that is really encouraging for the young players to know how much it still means to him.'

Unfortunately for Giggs, a slight hamstring injury left him unable to aid his colleagues as their season wandered into a stunning 6-1 home defeat to league leaders City, a result which left the second-placed Reds with a five-point gap to bridge and mental scars to heal. Absent for a run of seven games, as Ferguson's men rebuilt their confidence and momentum – during which time he became the Premier League's first winner of the Golden Foot and was inducted to Monte Carlo's 'Champions Promenade' (a footballing equivalent to Hollywood's Walk of Fame) – the Welshman returned for a trip to his homeland to face Swansea City, the first league game he'd ever played in the country of his birth. Sure enough, he pounced on a mistake from Angel Rangel to cross for Javier Hernandez to score the game's only goal, and was afforded a warm reception from the home support at the Liberty Stadium after his late substitution.

The Golden Foot award ensures more space is required in the Giggs trophy room.

Afterwards Giggs admitted: 'It was nice to play a league game in Wales. It was a long time coming. It's always nice to come home and I appreciated the ovation.'

Having won five games in a row after the derby debacle, United's resurgence was soon dented by draws against Benfica and Newcastle, followed by a League Cup exit at home to second-tier Crystal Palace. By the time of the shock defeat to the Londoners, football had been rocked by the unexpected death of Wales manager Gary Speed. As a former international colleague, Ryan was stunned. 'I am totally devastated,' he said in a statement issued to the press. 'Gary Speed was one of the nicest men in football and someone I am honoured to call a teammate and friend. Words cannot begin to describe how sad I feel at hearing this awful news. It goes without saying my thoughts are with his family at this tremendously sad time.'

Back on the field, United's fortunes continued to fluctuate, with their inexperience jarringly apparent in Switzerland, where defeat to Basel prompted an unexpected early elimination from the Champions League group stage. Giggs, who completed 90 minutes and did more than any United player in the pursuit of salvaging qualification, was singled out for praise amid a post-match critique from ITV pundit Roy Keane.

'People have talked about the young players – you've had Jones, Chris Smalling, Young coming in – everybody building them up, but they've got a lot to do. It's a reality check for some,' said the former United skipper. 'I'd be getting hold of some of those lads, saying: "You'd better buck up your ideas." I think their best player tonight was Ryan Giggs; that sums it up – he's thirty-seven or thirty-eight – you can't be depending on him. United got what they deserved.'

Once again, the collective reaction from Ferguson's squad was a positive one, posting four successive Premier League wins and scoring 16 times in the process – including a deflected effort from Giggs in a 5-0 win at Fulham to extend his record of scoring in every single

Premier League season – but a further slump followed as defeats to Blackburn Rovers and Newcastle United bookended the start of 2012. Seeking to bolster his squad's experience ahead of a looming FA Cup trip to the Etihad Stadium, Ferguson shocked football with a surprise enlistment – though Giggs, typically, was ahead of the game.

'I knew a few days beforehand,' smiled the Welshman, after the return of Paul Scholes was announced an hour before the Reds' FA Cup win at City. 'I thought he'd retired too early – a lot of people did. Scholesy probably thought he'd made up his mind and when you've done that, you can't really change it. But he was still the best in training with the Reserves, so he obviously felt he could still do it. Nobody was going to disagree with that and it was a massive boost when we found out he was coming back.'

The stats agreed. While struggling in the cup competitions – exiting the FA Cup at Anfield and the Europa League against Athletic Club from Bilbao – United won 11 and drew one of the next 12 Premier League games to take a firm hold of the title race. A key victory in the run came at Carrow Road in late February, and owed much to the timeless brilliance of Giggs and Scholes.

With the score level at 1-1, Scholes's first-half header having been cancelled out, Giggs responded to Norwich's late equaliser by moving into a support striker role and he immediately began fashioning chances. When they went begging, it was the Welshman who sprinted on to Young's fabulous cross to prod home an injury-time winner from close range and seal an invaluable victory on his 900th appearance for the club. 'It doesn't get any better than that,' he grinned afterwards.

In the eyes of many experts, however, it was getting better all the time for United's ageless veteran. 'What differentiates Ryan from a lot of athletes is his mental strength,' said United's head of fitness Tony Strudwick. 'He is fazed by nothing. His mental strength, particularly at key moments of games, can be match-winning for us. That makes him the go-to guy when we're under pressure, as we saw at Norwich.

'... [Ryan] doesn't just train, he practises ... [he] will still be there practising his free-kicks at the end of training, still there working on his game. If he isn't happy with his delivery or crosses after a game, he'll come in the following week and work on them.'

'But his mentality is just one of the pillars of his career. Another is his physique – Ryan is the perfect football athlete. He has a physical capacity that not many athletes possess. He uses less energy per stride, so he's a smoother, more efficient athlete. That allows him to get through the number of games he has, as does the way he eats and lives. He's an ideal professional.

'He also has the right support around him and the ability to work on his technique – he doesn't just train, he practises. Those who do – for example Cristiano Ronaldo, Scholes, Giggs – come in and grab a bag of balls and they'll work on their game. Some can do whatever the coach puts on for them, then go home and think about it. Practice is a bit more cerebral and, even at his age, Ryan will still be there practising his free-kicks at the end of training, still there working on his game. If he isn't happy with his delivery or crosses after a game, he'll come in the following week and work on them. The environment is there for him, but it's that desire and hunger to still want to improve.

**Tony Strudwick**
Manchester United

Demonstrating his enduring sense of occasion, Giggs marks his 900th club appearance with an invaluable last-gasp winner at Norwich City.

tournament will always be a massive disappointment for me – that will always remain. But I'm getting the chance now and I'm looking forward to that. It was something I never thought was going to happen. Ever since I got the chance to put my name forward for the Olympics, it's something I wanted to be a part of.'

For Giggs, the Olympic experience comprised poignant outings at Old Trafford and Cardiff's Millennium Stadium against Senegal and Uruguay respectively and a headed goal against United Arab Emirates at Wembley, before a familiar fate for a British team at a major tournament: a quarter-final exit on penalties. Though the skipper scored his kick, Daniel Sturridge's effort was saved to take South Korea into the semi-finals. 'We weren't good enough,' reflected Ryan. 'That is the bottom line. But I will look back on this experience with great pride. To captain the Great Britain side has been a privilege. Obviously it is disappointing to have lost like we did, but the overall experience has been nothing but positive.'

In Giggs's absence, United had sought to bounce back from the sapping end to 2011-12 with the high-profile capture of Arsenal captain Robin van Persie. Tellingly, Ferguson consulted the elder statesmen of his dressing room before making a move. 'The players at United never saw Robin as an intruder; the boss and I tested that before we made a move for him,' revealed then first-team coach Rene Meulensteen. 'We dropped Robin's name with Paul Scholes and Ryan Giggs. We said to them: "What would you think if Robin van Persie comes here?" They both said the same thing. They both thought it would be outrageous if Robin came to United, and later so did all the other players. The reason we discussed it with Ryan and Paul is because they stand for the culture of Manchester United in the dressing room. They keep that culture and protect it.

'With both Giggsy and Scholesy, they were very mindful of that, and they were hugely important for me in my role if I needed help to get something across to the other players. They made sure that things

Ryan finally samples a major tournament as he captains Great Britain at the 2012 Olympics.

happened. I knew always what I wanted when I was planning the training sessions and certain elements are always there, it's just the matter of how you package it and communicate it. I just needed to have a quiet word with one of those two to make sure that the things I wanted to come out were going to happen. I didn't need to address the whole group, I just had to have a word with one of them, and every single player listened to them.'

Van Persie and Japanese international Shinji Kagawa were soon among the squad of players listening to the dressing room's authority figures, and both new signings scored in Giggs's first start of the campaign, a 3-2 victory over Fulham. His second, a 3-2 triumph over Wigan, came on a day of milestones. Comparative pup Rio Ferdinand made his 400th appearance for the club, while Ryan made his 600th Premier League start and Scholes reached 700 outings in all competitions.

On a day made for nostalgia, the United manager couldn't help but cast an eye to the future. 'My personal feeling is that Ryan can play for another couple of years,' Ferguson proffered. 'It's a landmark for the three players and it's a great example to the younger players about what can be achieved if they sacrifice in football. These players have done that or they would never have got to this stage.

'You can't judge Ryan's performances at the moment because I haven't played him – but he will be involved in a lot of games this season, as normal, and I'm sure we'll see his ability. I'm lucky to have worked with both Ryan and Paul. It's not a matter of being proud to have had them. It's more a matter of saying: "I'm lucky to have had two devoted players like that." It's been brilliant.'

But while the emotional outpourings cascaded about him, Giggs continued to analyse his own form. Left frustrated by a poor performance against Tottenham, in which the visitors ploughed through United's centre at will and registered their first victory at Old Trafford for twenty-three years, the 38-year-old managed to find areas of his strict regime in which to further himself.

Sir Alex cited Ryan and fellow old heads Paul Scholes and Rio Ferdinand as examples of the benefits of sacrifice.

'The team were awful, but I was awful. I was down after that game. My thinking is: "What are you going to do about it?" It's just stupid things, like saying: "Right, I'm not going to have butter on my toast. I'm going to make sure I go to bed an hour earlier. I'm going to make sure I go home after every training session for a couple of weeks and rest my legs. I'm going to do extra running." There's no alcohol, certainly. My weight doesn't really fluctuate, but I make sure I don't eat late at night. It's about making sure I'm right physically because mentally I'm OK.'

Sure enough, Giggs's next start provided a jaw-dropping showcase of the benefits of such self-discipline. Three days after a substitute cameo in a rare Premier League win at Stamford Bridge – in which he was struck by a coin after Hernandez's late winner – he captained a much-changed Reds side for a League Cup fourth-round tie against a strong Blues side. Though there was ultimately heartbreak for the visitors, as Chelsea thrice came from behind to win 5-4 in extra time, Giggs opened and closed the scoring with a neat early finish and a penalty in the 120th minute.

'I think, in Ryan Giggs, we saw a player of unbelievable proportions, in terms of playing the 120 minutes at 39 years of age next month and it's a credit to himself,' admitted Ferguson. 'It's an example to every player on the pitch, even the Chelsea players.'

'It's tough to take,' shrugged the skipper. 'When you score four goals away from home, more often than not you win the game. I'm proud of the young players who played, though. You try to take the positives from a game like that, but there are a lot of disappointed lads and rightly so because they put in good performances. But they'll learn from it and the experience they'll gain from this is more than they could ever get from a Reserves game. Chelsea had to stick all their big guns on in the end to make an impact, which they did. As I said, though, I'm proud of the young players – they never stopped battling. We're just disappointed

After opening the scoring at Stamford Bridge, Ryan went on to complete 120 minutes – and score again – as the Reds were ousted from the League Cup in a nine-goal thriller.

to put on a good performance, score four goals and come away with nothing.'

Though he soon endured another below-par evening in a low-key Champions League defeat to CFR Cluj, Giggs remained a regular contributor as United set a devastating pace at the head of the Premier League table. By the turn of the year, the Reds led champions City by seven points, with summer recruit van Persie a free-scoring centrepiece in the team. As the Dutchman reflected on his first few months at Old Trafford, he volunteered special praise for his elder peers. 'I'm seeing small things that people don't see from the outside, which really make me happy,' said van Persie. 'For example, playing five against two in the box [a training drill with an emphasis on ball retention], and being with Scholesy and with Giggs. The choices they make in that box are just incredible. It's just great fun to be part of that. It makes me feel like I am surrounded by champions. I always knew that they were great players, but when you see them every day in training, or you're in the box with them, then you find out how good someone is. Scholesy and Giggsy are even better than I first expected.'

To emphasise the point, within days of van Persie's interview, he was on the receiving end of a phenomenal assist from Giggs which facilitated his late equaliser in an FA Cup third-round tie at West Ham. The pair had been introduced as second-half substitutes as the Reds sought to recover a 2-1 deficit and, on the cusp of injury time, Giggs dropped a pinpoint, half-volleyed pass into van Persie's path, 55 yards away. The Dutchman's silken take and uncompromising finish completed a goal of devastating simplicity.

'It was probably one of the goals of the season,' said the Welshman. 'We probably didn't use Robin as much as we should have in regards to the runs he was making, which is only natural when he's come to a new club and he's a different sort of player, but his runs off the shoulder are so intelligent. As soon as I saw him, I knew where he was going, so I tried to put it in his path, which I did, but the

The best player at 'boxes' in training? A prime contender, although Paul Scholes (left) also excelled at it.

Given just 12 minutes to preserve United's FA Cup hopes, Giggs tees up a stunning equaliser for Robin van Persie at Upton Park.

touch and the finish were just clinical. It's just something you do in training. Sometimes the pass comes off, sometimes it doesn't, but the special thing about it is that it came off in the game and it was such an important goal. So yeah, I was happy with the pass!'

Given just 12 minutes in which to make a difference, Giggs had played a major role in saving his side. His ability to impact as a substitute was a feature of the latter years of his career and, according to Meulensteen, marked out a man of football intelligence. 'He's the sort of guy who doesn't just sit on the bench, come on and say: "I'm on, what happens now?" He reads the game,' said the Dutchman. 'He made a difference. He had such vast experience that nothing was going to surprise him. He was able to pick out certain things where he thought: "If I come on, that's the sort of pass I'm going to look for."'

On from the start in the Reds' fourth-round tie against Fulham, Ryan required under three minutes to open the scoring from the penalty spot and tee up a 4-1 stroll. Having scored his first goal at Old Trafford in two years and four days, the 39-year-old duly repeated the trick just a fortnight later, slotting home against Everton to extend his record of netting in consecutive league seasons – a feat which now stood at twenty-three terms in a row.

Now in comparatively prolific form, Giggs went on to net in his next Premier League outing with the close-range clincher in a 2-0 win at Queens Park Rangers, but not before receiving a resounding validation of his career's work. Introduced as a substitute in a 1-1 draw at Real Madrid in the first leg of a thrilling Champions League second-round tie, the decorated star was afforded a standing ovation from all corners of the Bernabéu stadium.

'It was strange because you are going on the pitch and I was concentrating fully on trying to do well for the team and make an impact,' said Ryan. 'I did recognise it, but as I was concentrating on doing well in the game it wasn't until afterwards that I really thought about it. It was great for me and I thank the Real Madrid fans for the welcome they gave me. Going on to the pitch at a place like the Bernabéu and being clapped by the home fans is something special.'

The Madridistas were taking advantage of the chance to pay homage to Giggs's career, but his sights remained set forward and the 39-year-old penned another one-year deal – the seventh extension of his rolling contract – ahead of the second leg in Manchester. The news was predictably well received within the squad. 'He is Mr Manchester United,' said Michael Carrick. 'He sets the tone around the dressing room. He doesn't say an awful lot but when he does speak, everyone listens and everyone respects him. It leads on to the pitch. Not many people have lasted as long as Ryan. You have to take it year-by-year and see how your legs hold up. He is a one-off.'

Totalling his appearances with United, Wales and Great Britain, Giggs had reached 999 outings in the victory at Loftus Road. Ferguson considered his next deployment, and opted to rest his oldest player against Norwich City in order to have him fresh for the second-leg decider against Real. 'Only the best for the best,' the Scot would later note.

'A couple of days before the Norwich game, when the manager said he's going to leave me out altogether, you start thinking: "Right, I'm going to be involved against Madrid,"' said Ryan. 'As soon as I heard those words – "You're not involved with Norwich" – my mindset was straight: "I'm playing against Real Madrid and get prepared for that."'

Jose Mourinho's side would witness Giggs's readiness in all its glory, as he turned in a man-of-the-match performance across the midfield to overshadow all the younger stars on show in both sides. It would ultimately be Ronaldo who had the last laugh, scoring the winner after United had been reduced to ten men by the controversial dismissal of Nani, but the former Reds winger saved the last word for his former colleague. 'Giggsy is the flag of his club,' said Ronaldo. 'I think he'll retire when he's fifty!'

There would be no such jocularity in the home dressing room, however, as Giggs sat in a sombre silence. 'It was quiet and two or

'Every training session, with the way he trains and loves the game, he sets the example for every single one of us, for old and for young. ... he's just unbelievable in training and during games. He's thirty-nine now but you can't tell. He's fit and he works his socks off.'

**Robin van Persie**
Manchester United

three times I went to say something like: "Make sure we win the FA Cup and league now," but I didn't,' he revealed. 'I just sat there for ten minutes. It didn't feel right to speak. It was a quiet moment.'

It wouldn't remain quiet for too much longer. Though Chelsea ousted United from the FA Cup quarter-final after a replay, the Reds had built an insurmountable lead in the title race and the inevitable was confirmed against Aston Villa with four games to spare. On an unforgettable evening at Old Trafford, Giggs supplied two-thirds of van Persie's hat-trick as the Reds wrapped up their twentieth domestic rule in style.

Though the Dutchman took the plaudits, he and several of his colleagues took the time to salute Giggs's sustained contribution. 'It is an honour for me to play and train with him. It really is. I told him as well,' said van Persie. 'Every training session, with the way he trains and loves the game, he sets the example for every single one of us, for old and for young. The way he plays, today he gave me two brilliant assists and, every single day, he's just unbelievable in training

Sharing a joke with Sir Alex Ferguson and the press as United prepare for another key Champions League battle.

Former colleague Cristiano Ronaldo, starring for Real Madrid, would end the Reds' European hopes, but it was man of the match Giggs who most caught the eye.

and during games. He's thirty-nine now but you can't tell. He's fit and he works his socks off. He is a true example for young and old.'

Coerced into chatting with Sky Sports after the game, the thirteen-time champion – a tally the equal of Arsenal and beaten only by United and Liverpool – saluted his club's reaction to the previous campaign's shock denouement. 'It's obviously special,' said Giggs. 'When you lose it in the manner that we did last year, to win it back is something special, especially by putting on a show in the first half. We did it in style.'

The veteran star also praised the influence of his manager, enthusing: 'His appetite is second to none. Every day at the training ground he's the first there, his enthusiasm is brilliant and that feeds through the club; he is the club. Everything comes from the manager, getting players in, getting the right staff in, and he's just an unbelievable manager and an unbelievable person and he deserves everything that he gets. He works hard and I've been very lucky to play under him for so long.'

Unbeknown to the Welshman, that staggeringly successful relationship was about to come to an end. A fortnight after clinching the title against Villa, Ferguson confirmed his decision to retire – a verdict also reached for a second time by Scholes – ahead of the final home game of the season, against Swansea. 'Sunday is about everyone who has shared in the journey – it should be a celebratory occasion,' insisted Giggs.

A winning finale at Old Trafford was secured by a narrow 2-1 win over the Swans. Giggs joined from the bench, as he did in a baffling 5-5 last-day draw at West Brom in which a 5-2 lead was squandered. The final goal of Ferguson's epic, 26-and-a-half year reign was scored by Chicharito and, fittingly, provided by an inviting Giggs cross. Rarely one to show emotion, it was the Welshman who persuaded Ferguson to break away from his players at the end of the game to partake in a mutual show of appreciation between the travelling supporters and their outgoing manager.

'It has been hard, it has been tough, especially for the players who have known him for a long time,' Giggs admitted after the

Ryan chases Robin van Persie after the Dutchman's stunning volley against Aston Villa brings title No. 20 sharply into focus.

Urged by Ryan to address the away fans at West Brom, Sir Alex says his farewells after his final game in charge.

subsequent trophy parade. 'But I am happy and delighted that we could end on a high by winning the league in his last season.'

With David Moyes already announced as Ferguson's successor, United were braced for a period of change. Having outlasted his manager and all his 1992 classmates, Giggs would remain as the embodiment of United's modern-day glories.

## Most Premier League Appearances

| Name | Debut | Farewell | Total |
|------|-------|----------|-------|
| Ryan Giggs | 15 August 1992 | 6 May 2014 | 632 |
| Frank Lampard | 31 January 1996 | 4 May 2014 | 577* |
| David James | 16 August 1992 | 1 May 2010 | 572 |
| Gary Speed | 15 August 1992 | 9 December 2007 | 534 |
| Gareth Barry | 2 May 1998 | 11 May 2014 | 531* |
| Emile Heskey | 8 Mar 1995 | 13 May 2012 | 517 |
| Jamie Carragher | 11 January 1997 | 19 May 2013 | 508 |
| Mark Schwarzer | 15 August 1998 | 11 May 2014 | 508* |
| Phil Neville | 11 February 1995 | 10 February 2013 | 505 |
| Sol Campbell | 5 December 1992 | 19 March 2011 | 503 |

*Correct to the end of the 2013-14 season.

## Top Ten Appearances for Manchester United

| Name | Debut | Farewell | Total |
|------|-------|----------|-------|
| Ryan Giggs | 2 March 1991 | 6 May 2014 | 963 |
| Bobby Charlton | 6 October 1956 | 28 April 1973 | 758 |
| Paul Scholes | 21 September 1994 | 19 May 2013 | 718 |
| Bill Foulkes | 13 December 1952 | 17 May 1969 | 688 |
| Gary Neville | 16 September 1992 | 1 January 2011 | 602 |
| Alex Stepney | 17 September 1966 | 29 April 1978 | 539 |
| Tony Dunne | 15 October 1960 | 17 February 1973 | 535 |
| Denis Irwin | 18 August 1990 | 11 May 2002 | 529 |
| Joe Spence | 30 August 1919 | 1 April 1933 | 510 |
| Arthur Albiston | 9 October 1974 | 13 February 1988 | 485 |

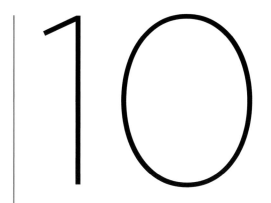

# A Twist in the Tale

The aftershocks of Sir Alex Ferguson's departure undermined the stability that had underpinned Giggs's illustrious stay at United. The Scot could not go on forever and his retirement prompted an unavoidably daunting step into the unknown for everybody who had grown accustomed to years of unparalleled success, including a player in the twilight of his career.

Ferguson accepted a position on the board while his fellow countryman David Moyes asked Giggs to join his coaching team, working alongside Steve Round, Phil Neville and Jimmy Lumsden. There was a sense that the Welshman's priority would remain his onfield commitments, but the move would assist in ushering in the new backroom team and making the transition as painless as possible.

'This club has had the same manager for nearly twenty-seven years,' stated Phil Neville on his return to Manchester. 'There's going to

be slightly different training sessions, slight changes in style, and Ryan can help with that changeover period.'

Ferguson, Moyes and the new player-coach met at an Alderley Edge hotel to discuss the future and, after the initial contact was made during a stay in Turkey to work on his coaching badges, Giggs had mulled it over and felt he could not reject the opportunity to influence the direction the club was taking.

The initial signs were positive in terms of the first impressions he made on the training pitch, indicating a determination to impress the new boss. 'Some of the stuff he does every day, you just marvel at,' enthused Moyes. 'Having seen him at close quarters and got to work with him, I can't imagine how good he must have been in his prime.'

After admitting Giggs was even better than he had envisaged as an outsider, Moyes selected him in his first competitive line-up for the Community Shield against Wigan Athletic. A 2-0 triumph clinched what would be his final piece of silverware and the Welshman also played for 67 minutes of the opening-day victory at Swansea City. Although the team had failed to sparkle in pre-season, perhaps things would run more smoothly than anticipated after all, even if a taxing fixture schedule loomed large on the horizon.

Giggs featured in a 0-0 draw with a Chelsea side reunited with Jose Mourinho, while a 1-0 loss at Liverpool was at least avenged, in part, by knocking the Merseysiders out of the Capital One Cup, with Ryan completing the full 90 minutes for the first time under the new regime and still looking in fine fettle.

His longevity was starting to throw up incredible generational anomalies. Jordan Henderson, who was in direct opposition in midfield in both of those matches against Brendan Rodgers' team, spoke of a holiday photograph he had taken when he was a three-year-old on a Majorcan beach with the famous United winger. 'I remember it vaguely, but I was really young,' said the England international. 'I don't think he'd recall it at all!'

The post-Ferguson era began with more silverware, but the 2013 Community Shield would be the final trophy of Giggs's playing career.

Welcome to the other side of the touchline. Jose Mourinho returns to Old Trafford as Chelsea manager to find Ryan lining up in the opposite dugout.

# Ryan Giggs
## The Man for All Seasons

Jack Barmby trained with the first-teamers at the Aon Training Complex before joining Hartlepool United on loan and signing for Leicester City in the summer of 2014. 'My dad was with Giggsy at Lilleshall, so obviously they know each other well,' he stated. 'Everyone says it but you have to see how Ryan trains – it's the way he plays. He is great to look up to because you think he is that good because of the way he is in training and the way he conducts himself.'

Thomas Ince, who shared a room with the United winger when he lodged at the Ince family home in the 1990s, came up against his idol later in the season when representing Crystal Palace. Belgian prodigy Adnan Januzaj, making waves after his own breakthrough in 2013-14, was born eight months after Giggs had already won a league title and the Double. Yet, for all the fear that time was catching up with him, the Welshman lost none of the hunger to pull on the red shirt.

Although Moyes initially decided the experience of his player-coach was essential, the domestic games dried up for the veteran. He came off the bench in three matches in October and November, including a narrow 1-0 success over leaders Arsenal which briefly reignited hopes of a championship challenge, but Giggs would enjoy more involvement in European competition.

After coming off the bench in Ukraine against Shakhtar Donetsk, he started the four remaining Champions League group games and excelled in a resounding 5-0 thrashing of Bayer Leverkusen. He played a major part goals for Antonio Valencia and Chris Smalling. 'Actually during the game, the Bayer centre-half was asking how Ryan is still playing at that age,' revealed Wayne Rooney. 'I certainly won't be playing at that age. His composure on the ball is great.'

Giggs's 40th birthday celebrations included his teammates all wearing masks of his face and pinning up posters of his younger days that made him cringe with embarrassment. He had joked he would stay in bed to avoid anything the players had planned for him, even if

Having learned his trade under the wing of Bryan Robson and other senior pros, Ryan swaps roles and looks after twinkling talents such as Adnan Januzaj.

'He's really a shining light to any professional out there ... In terms of actual coaching ... he works a lot on the forwards and wide players, but he has to prepare himself to play as well. He's got the balance just right .... He still gets changed in the first-team dressing room but he's a coach. He's got that bit of class and experience to handle that.'

**Phil Neville**
Manchester United

nothing could be further from the truth. 'He's in doing his yoga in the mornings,' revealed Moyes. 'He is in before anybody at the club.'

Unfortunately, setbacks were just around the corner as his next outing was a costly home reverse to Moyes's former club Everton, only their third league win at Old Trafford since Ryan's debut, and the lack of a settled side hampered any bid for a sustained run of form. He returned to the fray for wins at Aston Villa and Norwich City, but was withdrawn at the interval for match-winner Danny Welbeck at Carrow Road.

Phil Neville touched on the difficulties his friend faced for still seeing himself as a player, rather than a coach, as the minutes on the field, the very lifeblood of any footballer, were being restricted. 'I'd say 90 per cent of his work is still as a player,' said Neville. 'I've got to say he's been fantastic still in training and playing. He's really a shining light to any professional out there, but he does have a big influence in the coaching room. In terms of actual coaching, most of mine and Giggsy's work is probably done on an individual basis. Ryan, in particular, works a lot on the forwards and wide players, but he has to prepare himself to play as well. He's got the balance just right and I'd say he's handling it really well. He still gets changed in the first-team dressing room but he's a coach. He's got that bit of class and experience to handle that.'

With ambitions being recalibrated as the league title defence instead became a quest for a top-four spot and Champions League qualification, there was at least the hope of some salvation in the form of the Capital One Cup. On a luckless night in the semi-final first leg at the Stadium of Light, Giggs's 90 minutes included rattling Vito Mannone's bar and scoring the only own goal of his career, when challenging former colleague Phil Bardsley to a Wes Brown cross. Sunderland would deny the Reds an all-Manchester final with City by winning a penalty shoot-out after the second leg.

A first league appearance for a month came in a 2-0 victory over his home town Cardiff City and he came off the bench at Crystal Palace for 10 minutes in February, but Ryan was clearly and understandably frustrated by the time the Champions League round of 16 second leg with Olympiacos approached. Arguably the nadir of United's poor season had occurred in Piraeus when a 2-0 reverse threatened to prematurely end interest in another competition. The Reds had performed well in the group stages but were dreadful in the Greek capital and required a comeback at Old Trafford akin to the memorable triumph against Barcelona in the European Cup-Winners' Cup 30 years previously.

Robin van Persie may have scored all three goals without reply, but Giggs proved a point – he was still very much capable of controlling the tempo of matches and creating opportunities for the forwards; the Dutchman's first two goals came from his passes. 'I just

say that he is a freak of nature,' opined Moyes. 'It wasn't as if I thought he was tiring after 60 minutes and he's not played for a month or two. His performance was up there with as well as he's played in my time that I've been here.'

The display prompted as many questions as answers for the manager. 'Ryan can't go on forever,' countered Moyes, when asked why he had not selected him more often. 'We know that. We have to be looking to find the new Ryan Giggs and the new players. He is forty years old and I needed to look to the future, to give people opportunities to play.'

Ahead of the quarter-final against Bayern Munich, Giggs sat alongside Moyes to preview the game at the press conference. He spoke with the authority of a figure steeped in United's values. 'We don't see ourselves as underdogs,' he rallied. 'We see ourselves as Manchester United playing at home in the Champions League and we can't wait.' It was a statesmanlike performance and drew praise from the watching media. His words were measured and there was a positivity that raised expectations, even if the Reds would eventually succumb late in the second leg in Bavaria.

The stellar showing against Olympiacos earned him a start against Bayern, but the clock was already ticking down on his playing career. The sublime display in the previous round would be the last game he ever completed. He was replaced at half time against the reigning European champions by Shinji Kagawa in his final start for the club. It was also the last time Moyes would pick him, as the manager lost his job after a defeat at his former employers Everton ended any hopes of finishing in the top four.

Moyes understandably wanted to allow all of his squad a chance to prove their worth, hence the remarkable statistic that he fielded different starting XIs in all 51 fixtures during his short time in charge. Statistics seldom tell the full story, but of United's 16 defeats in 2013-14, Ryan played in only three, and one of those was a retrievable

Robin van Persie completes his hat-trick in a famous victory over Olympiacos, a game in which the outstanding Giggs completed 90 minutes for the final time.

Watched on by under-pressure David Moyes, Ryan explains to the world's media why European champions Bayern Munich should hold no fear for United.

situation in the Capital One Cup semi-finals. Of his 22 outings, 13 were victories. He was still influencing games and will argue his form warranted more regular involvement.

If being named a coach came earlier than expected, then the board's decision to hand Giggs the manager's job on an interim basis was certainly way ahead of schedule. His head was in a spin when offered the promotion, but he quickly focused on preparing for the final four games of the season, ironically ending his hopes of having a major impact in a playing capacity.

It was a whirlwind period for Ryan. Kath Phipps, the receptionist at the Aon Training Complex, is one of the few people at United whose longevity extends beyond his arrival at the club. 'You've come a long way from the scruffy 13-year-old kid I first met,' she told him and the newly anointed interim boss duly provided an emotional hug as the magnitude of the achievement hit home.

The task in hand was an enormous one and yet he handled it with aplomb, dealing with the press conferences and interviews like the seasoned campaigner he has become. 'I've just given myself a five-year contract,' he joked as he astutely handled any awkward questions about the situation regarding the former manager. The mood was lifted and the club seemed more relaxed with the fans heralding his appearance from the tunnel, bedecked in a suit, for his first game in charge against Norwich City.

'I've got to say it's the proudest moment of my life,' he revealed. The reception from the crowd emphasised their affection and own pride at seeing him lead the team out against the Canaries. The side responded with a 4-0 victory, but the honeymoon period was short lived as a 0-1 reverse to Sunderland brought everybody back down to earth with a bump.

Giggs was furious with the players and felt they had let themselves down, even if the Black Cats had far more to play for in staving off relegation. He was learning on the job and reverted to

'The proudest moment of my life,' says Giggs, as his four-game stint as interim manager begins against Norwich City at Old Trafford.

instinct for the visit of Hull City, naming himself on the bench for the first time since taking over the reins to raise hopes of one final outing before hanging up his boots. Just as pertinently, he pinned his faith in youth, starting with debutants Tom Lawrence and James Wilson to send out a strong signal regarding his ethos.

'Maybe he was putting a marker down,' said youth coach Tony Whelan. '"I can set these kids on course for the first team." It is a big statement that, in terms of what he thinks about giving young players an opportunity to play. He got one when his manager had the confidence to do that with him. He was doing the same and it was a great boost to those young boys.

'You don't know what will happen until you try them. It's like jumping out of an aeroplane or anything else. If you don't try it, you will never know. It's all about the stepping stones and following the footsteps of the Busby Babes – all the way back to those days. To see it being carried on through Ryan is fantastic. The club should never change this legacy. We have all got the privilege to be bequeathed as guardians of these traditions and to have Ryan on board as another guardian of it is amazing.'

Wilson scored twice in the 3-1 triumph against Steve Bruce's Tigers to fully vindicate the interim manager and announce his own arrival in dramatic fashion. 'He talked to me and just said: "Play your own game, I'm going to put you straight in,"' revealed the 18-year-old striker. 'So I had the morning to get my head around it and definitely preferred it that way because you can get into the mindset of what you're going to do in the game.

'He was trying to do what Sir Alex did in bringing youth through by giving you that chance on the pitch. I did my best. I was definitely nervous but, to be fair, he tried to reassure me. I was going to ask him if he was nervous the first time he played, just to receive a bit of advice, but I thought I'd better let him get on with doing his job. I do know I can go to him for advice on something like that. I just felt,

Having handed untried talent James Wilson his debut against Hull City, the interim manager watches the youngster bag a brace of goals.

Fellow Welshman Tom Lawrence – another debutant – makes way for the boss, who takes to the Old Trafford turf for the final time.

on this occasion, it was best to let him concentrate on managing the team.'

Lawrence was asked if he benefited from being a fellow Welshman. 'I suppose it can only help!' laughed the talented forward. 'He just said I would be involved and I thought I might come on as a substitute or something like that. Obviously, it was encouraging he thought I could take my game to the next level. It showed he has it in him to make such bold decisions because he didn't care what other people thought.'

The night was very nearly a perfect one. Lawrence entered the record books by being replaced by Giggs on his final appearance, the only regret for the young pair being that they never shared the pitch at the same time as the legend who commands their respect. 'It was an amazing thing to happen,' admitted Lawrence. 'It was a shame [to come off] but it was the only downfall.' Wilson added: 'I didn't get the privilege to play on the same pitch as him, but being around while he's been here has been brilliant with his experience and the way he is around us youngsters.'

Ryan had been scrutinising the action from the touchline while warming up, a peculiar spectacle as the future wrestled with the present. There was a romantic element to seeing him take to the field for one last time, creating the clinching goal for van Persie with an astute pass to register one final assist. 'Nobody else before had played that pass in the game,' commented former United coach Rene Meulensteen. 'Everything was going in a banana shape. That's the quality of vision and the confidence to hit a ball like that. Not many have that.'

Hull keeper Eldin Jakupovic denied him the ultimate last hurrah, diving to push away a free-kick that would have brought the house down. The sheepish Bosnian even made an apology to the Stretford End behind him, after ending Giggs's record of having scored in every Premier League season, but at least there was an opportunity

Ryan goes agonisingly close to scoring for the 24th season in a row, but his free-kick is fended away by Tigers goalkeeper Eldin Jakupovic.

Signing off for the season at Old Trafford, Giggs addresses a packed stadium after the 3-1 victory over Hull.

to see the Welshman grace the big stage one last time. He took the microphone at the end, as Sir Alex always did following the last home game of the season, and the realisation that the greatest British club career of all time was, in all likelihood, ending dawned on Old Trafford.

It was 963 and out for Giggs. He retired as a player having totally exceeded all expectations, no matter how high they had been when he wowed everybody as a schoolboy and earned those comparisons with George Best. Although confirmation of the decision would not be made until the summer, any comment would now forever refer to his footballing ability in the past tense. 'I'd like to be remembered, first and foremost, as the footballer who loved playing for United,' he said. 'For the way I played. I tried to entertain, score goals and create goals.'

> 'I'd like to be remembered, first and foremost, as the footballer who loved playing for United ... For the way I played. I tried to entertain, score goals and create goals.'

**Ryan Giggs**
Manchester United

Back in 1993, the erudite writer Hunter Davies penned a piece in the *Sunday Times* articulating his fears for what the next two decades would hold for the youngster. 'Will Ryan turn into George in twenty years?' he pondered. 'Will that sweet, adolescent Celtic face grow Latino swarthy and become knowing and clever, cynical and seen-it-all? At present, he has no waist, no spare flesh and no discernible muscles. The time will come, with a hardening of the arteries and the attitudes, and we will look at his grown-up phizog and wonder where that frail little boy went. What the future holds for him as a player, that's the real worry. That's where our fears lie. I hope it will be a case of perfect temperament, perfect skills, a career perfectly fulfilled. No other words will then be needed. We'll have the pictures in our head.'

Davies, who penned autobiographies for Paul Gascoigne, Wayne Rooney and Dwight Yorke, admitted he is relieved to have those 'pictures' stored in the memory bank as he revisited those words in the wake of Giggs's retirement. 'He is one of my heroes,' said the author. 'It's typical in football for people to not keep progressing forever, but Giggs's curve has been upward really all his life.

'I always think players should go abroad for a change of culture and training because it will shake them up and teach them new things. Considering Ryan has stayed at one club all his life, personally, I think that's a handicap as it blocks development. But he has flourished and done brilliantly. He was ahead of his time and always seemed to be health conscious. He was sensible with his diet and also tracked back to defend. In the old days, wingers didn't defend. I don't think Chris Waddle and David Ginola ever went back in their own half.'

The less glamorous side of the game had certainly always been embraced by a player with a tremendous team ethic, as both Denis Irwin and Patrice Evra will attest. 'Throughout all the time we played together, Ryan was my left foot,' recalled Irwin. 'He wasn't afraid to do his defensive duties. He would always do the dirty side of things. I could always trust him to come back and mark the overlapping full-back. He made my job a hell of a lot easier.'

Not many superstars of the game, blessed with his flair and sense of adventure, would show such diligence. It had made him the complete package as a footballer. 'I was at a dinner celebrating the twenty-fifth anniversary of the [1968] European Cup win,' revealed Brian Kidd, who helped nurture this remarkable talent. 'I was on the top table for a question-and-answer session with Sir Bobby, Paddy Crerand

and Alex Stepney. They were talking about the great players going back to the tragedy of Munich.

'It came to my turn and it was mentioned to me about all the legendary players of the past and I turned around and said you must put Ryan Giggs on that list. He could certainly hold his own with that elite group.'

There was still one final match as interim manager, with the Reds drawing 1-1 at Southampton in a low-key affair on the final day of a disappointing campaign. As rumours increased that Netherlands coach Louis van Gaal would be United's next permanent manager after the summer's World Cup, there was an anxious wait for supporters to hear confirmation that Ryan would remain as part of any new regime.

In the interim, he received the inaugural lifetime achievement award at the club's end-of-season gala dinner, where a galaxy of greats paid tribute on a special MUTV film screened to a bashful Giggs and the audience. Over time, the superlatives which remained unused about him steadily diminished, but Gary Neville raised a laugh by joking: 'I sometimes wonder how someone has the confidence and the belief to have gone on so long but I suppose, running at me and Phil every single day in training, I'd have played on until I was forty!'

Real Madrid's Cristiano Ronaldo acknowledged the part his fellow winger had paid in his development into the best player on the planet. 'It was a pleasure for me to play with you at United,' said the Portugal superstar. 'I remember I was eighteen and it was an unbelievable feeling to play with you. I learned a lot from you.'

Giggs – the player – also leaves that legacy for youngsters that will stand the club in great stead for future generations. He is the benchmark for marrying innate talent with insatiable desire for success through sheer hard work and dedication on the training ground.

Ryan receives the club's inaugural lifetime achievement award from Sir Bobby Charlton at the end of the 2013-14 campaign.

'It's not just about Ryan's God-given talent with his balance, it's the fact he's utilised that and made the most of it by playing until forty,' explained Reserves coach Warren Joyce, who worked closely with the Welshman during his spell in interim charge. 'It's the way you lead your life with the habits that you possess. If he can pass that on to any young players and bottle it, that is a massive gift as a coach, to make them like he is. That's regardless of anything else – technical or tactical – it's about trying to be the best they can. When you have been the best you can be for twenty-three years over almost a thousand games, that's the secret and a huge lesson to pass on to any youngsters.

'Loyalty has been a big part of the tradition and history of the club and he is steeped in that,' Joyce added. 'All great players will have the same character traits as Ryan. You must have discipline in your life, be humble, work hard and remain loyal to the club. They are the things you want all young players to emulate.'

As a role model for any schoolboy first walking through the doors of the Aon Training Complex, there is nobody better. Gary Neville, Paul Scholes and other one-club men are the examples that fledgling footballers can aspire to follow. 'It's something almost exclusive to our club, something we're proud of and something that gives us a great advantage when attracting young players,' explained Sir Alex, who would soon see another man at the helm he had tended so steadily for so long.

Van Gaal was finally confirmed as United's next manager on 19 May, the same day that Giggs confirmed his retirement in order to focus on a new role as the Dutchman's assistant manager. 'It was a very easy conversation to have [with van Gaal] about Ryan,' disclosed executive vice-chairman Ed Woodward. 'He said he wanted Ryan to be in his group. It's very important to us as a club that we have continuity and Ryan is the perfect person to continue that continuity. He did a great job in the set-up last year and has obviously been at the club for a long time, so we're very pleased about that.'

There were many, including former chief executive David Gill, who felt it was imperative to retain somebody ingrained in the club with the potential to become manager on a full-time basis. Learning from van Gaal would surely be beneficial in achieving that goal.

'I'm absolutely thrilled he is staying on,' said board member Gill. 'I think he will be very useful to the new manager in terms of knowing the history and what Manchester United is all about. At the same time, he can learn from our new manager and develop his career to new heights on the managerial front. It's something I'm sure he can achieve.

'It's been quite interesting hearing people like Jose Mourinho talking about what he learned under Sir Bobby Robson at Barcelona. To work under the new man will be very important for Ryan and a great bridge from playing at the highest level for so many years to developing a career in management.

'It's a great opportunity as assistant manager. It's ideal and I think the important thing is he's not been given it just because we're merely treating him right. Louis van Gaal has clearly seen something in him after watching him for years and realises: "This guy can win things for me." Ryan has got that British sense of humour, the camaraderie and spirit which is important for the dressing room. It's a different role for him there and he is going to have to wear his new hat clearly but, at the same time, people respect him and he can be that prominent appointment with the ethos of Manchester United. As someone coming in, I'm sure Mr van Gaal read things in books and watched United, but it is not the same as having that experience of the club, so Ryan will help him in that respect.'

Giggs effectively remained in charge while the Dutchman focused on taking the Netherlands to third place at the World Cup in Brazil. Ryan found time to complete more coaching badges and undertake some South African television punditry work on the World Cup while also keeping things ticking over at the club. He will be a key figure in the new coaching set-up and nobody will be more

▼

A new chapter. Having confirmed his retirement, Giggs accepts a role as assistant manager under newly appointed Louis van Gaal.